Institutions, Transition Economies, and Economic Development

Institutions, Transition Economies, and Economic Development

Timothy J. Yeager

Westview Press
A Member of the Perseus Books Group

HR
82
.Y4
1999

Political Economy of Global Interdependence

Copyright © 1999 by Westview Press, A member of the Perseus Books Group

Published in 1998 in the United States of America by Westview Press, 5500 Central Avenue, Boulder, Colorado 80301-2877, and in the United Kingdom by Westview Press, 12 Hid's Copse Road, Cumnor Hill, Oxford OX2 9JJ

A CIP catalog record for this book is available from the Library of Congress.
ISBN 0-8133-3572-8 (hc)—ISBN 0-8133-3573-6 (pb)

The paper used in this publication meets the requirements of the American National Standard for Permanence of Paper for Printed Library Materials Z39.48-1984.

10   9   8   7   6   5   4   3   2   1

To my wife Dara,
and my children, Rachel, Mitch, and Rebecca.
Thank you for all your love and support

Contents

Tables and Figures

Preface

A nation's institutional framework is the most important factor determining its economic performance through time. Yet in economic theory, the role of institutions has been treated superficially at best and most often ignored completely. Recently research in the fields of institutions, transaction costs, and information has rapidly been working its way into "mainstream" economics. A revolution in economic theory is under way, one that will permanently expand the way that economists think about the performance of real-world economies.

One of my reasons for studying economics was to understand the huge disparity in standards of living across countries. As a graduate student, I sat through many economic theory courses discussing Pareto efficiency and various versions of Rational Expectations models. I had a sense that what I was learning was not applicable to a real-world economy. Furthermore, these theories contributed nothing whatsoever to my understanding of economic disparities across countries. Then I took Douglass North's course on the New Institutional Economics. This theory of institutions and its conception of the role that institutions play in determining economic performance seemed grounded in reality and went to the heart of my questions.

I was excited about what I was learning. Economics as a social science was now able to convincingly explain real-world events. Ever since, as an instructor, I have attempted to integrate the New Institutional Economics into my classes. This has not been an easy task. The main obstacle is that there is no book on institutions written specifically for undergraduate students. This book fills that gap. It is intended for use in upper-level undergraduate courses in any course on institutions, economic development, transition studies, or comparative economic systems. Because the book is targeted primarily to undergraduates, difficult economic concepts are explained thoroughly. However, the book's readership need not be limited to undergraduates and academics. It can be read and easily understood by anyone interested in the question of why some nations are wealthy while most are poor.

The New Institutional Economics provides a broad theoretical framework for analyzing and explaining economic performance. Despite some claims to the contrary, this theory is not an alternative to mainstream neoclassical economic theory. Rather, it builds upon existing neoclassical economics. The New Institutional Economics is much broader in scope and capable of explaining more economic events. It is analogous to Keynes's critique of classical macroeconomics, in which he argued that the classical equilibrium outcome of full employment was but one of many possible equilibria. Likewise, institutionalists argue that the Pareto-efficient outcome of neoclassical economics is but one of many possible outcomes. An economy will only achieve the efficient outcome under certain institutional arrangements.

The New Institutional Economics allows us to simultaneously analyze such diverse topics as transitions from socialism to capitalism and economic development. This book shows that the goals of both transition economies and developing economies are the same. Both types of economy must create an institutional framework that lowers transaction costs and creates incentives for dynamic efficiency. The major difference between the two is that transition economies must create capitalist market institutions from the ground up, whereas most developing economies already have a base from which to build.

This book takes the reader through the main elements of the New Institutional Economics and then applies that theory to transition and developing economies. I explore the merger of East and West Germany, the transition experiences of Poland and Russia, and the developing economies of Mexico and South Korea, and the book concludes with an analysis of China and the recent integration of Hong Kong.

Timothy J. Yeager

Acknowledgments

I wish to thank Doug North, whose theories and ideas provided me with the inspiration for this project. As time will tell, the New Institutional Economics will continue to spread through the economics profession. Doug also generously gave his time to review an early version of the manuscript. I owe Ben French, my research assistant and good friend, a big debt for doing many thankless tasks such as digging up references and data from the library. I also wish to thank Steve Hackett, my colleague when I was at Humboldt State University. He helped me to think clearly about my target audience, and provided support and encouragement along the way. Most of this book was written while I was an assistant professor of economics at Humboldt State University. I owe the university a great debt, and I will always treasure the memories of my wonderful experience there and the bonds that I made with my colleagues in the business school.

The views expressed here are solely the views of the author, not necessarily those of the Federal Reserve Bank of St. Louis or the Federal Reserve system.

T.J.Y.

1

Introduction

Economic Growth

Some nations are very wealthy. Most nations are poor. Is there latent potential in developing economies that would allow them to prosper? If so, what is the key to unlocking that wealth potential? Economics is primarily concerned with material standards of living. People derive satisfaction and enjoyment from the goods and services they consume. The average person in the United States has luxuries at his disposal that kings in ancient times could not have imagined. We dress in comfortable clothing and have a whole wardrobe to choose from, depending on the weather and the social function we are attending. We have running hot water, heating, and air conditioning. We are able to travel great distances in short periods in trains, automobiles, and airplanes. We have aspirin to relieve headaches. We can visit dentists to care for our teeth and doctors to cure our kids' ear infections. We have access to constant entertainment through television, radio, movies, and, more recently, the Internet. Most of these revolutions have occurred within the past century. Consequently, in a very real sense the average person in the United States lives better than a king. The more we are able to consume, the higher our material standards of living.

Standards of living vary considerably across countries. Table 1.1 lists gross national product (GNP) per capita in 1997 and other economic indicators for selected countries. GNP is the money value of all final goods and services produced by a country's citizens in a given year. GNP *per capita* is GNP divided by the country's population. A more common and very similar measure of a nation's economy is gross domestic product (GDP). GDP is the money value of all final goods and services produced within a nation's borders in a given year. GDP differs from GNP in that it excludes any production abroad by domestic citizens, yet it does count production by foreign entities in the country. A country's level of production is roughly equal to its level of income, because all revenue from

TABLE 1.1   Basic Economic Indicators

Country	GNP per Capita[a]	Population[b]	Population Density[c]	Education[d]	Income Distribution (Gini index)	Share of Income to Highest 10%
U.S.	28,740	268	29	97.5	45	28.5
Switzerland	26,320	7	175	91	29	28.6
Japan	23,400	126	334	96	17	22.4
Hong Kong	22,950	6.2	6,200	N/A	N/A	31.3
France	21,860	59	107	105.5	43	26.1
Canada	21,680	30	3	103.5	36	24.1
Germany	21,300	82	235	100.5	N/A	24.4
S. Korea	13,500	46	465	92.5	38.9	N/A
Argentina	9,950	36	13	72.5	N/A	N/A
Mexico	8,120	95	50	57.5	50.3	39.2
S. Africa	7,490	38	31	77.5	58.4	47.3
Poland	6,380	39	128	84.5	27.2	22.1
Brazil	6,240	164	19	N/A	63.4	51.3
Russia	4,190	147	9	87.5	49.6	38.7
China	3,570	1,227	132	55.5	37.6	26.8
India	1,650	961	323	48.5	33.8	28.4
Haiti	1,150	7	250	N/A	N/A	N/A
Nigeria	880	118	130	29.5	36.1	31.3

[a] 1997 GNP per capita, adjusted for purchasing power parity using current international dollars.
[b] Mid-year 1997 estimates in millions.
[c] People per square kilometer.
[d] Average of male and female enrollment rates.
SOURCES: *World Development Report* (New York: Oxford University Press, 1998), pp. 190–191, *World Development Report,* 1997, pp. 214–215, 222–223, 226–227.

production eventually is paid out as income. The income might be paid as wages or salaries, as interest or rent to the owners of machinery, or as profits to the owners of the firm. Therefore, GDP per capita is approximately equal to income per capita. This measure is a good proxy for the average material standard of living of a nation's citizens.

There are serious problems with this measure, however. First, GDP measures only production, not consumption. If a nation produces more nuclear bombs, the average consumer does not feel any better off even though GDP rises. Second, GDP does not measure many things that tell us about the *quality* of life. GDP very poorly reflects the state of the environment, for example. If massive deforestation occurs in a country, the GDP likely *increases* from the lumber production. Furthermore, GDP fails to account for the impact of crime (except that GDP rises when more prisons are built), the stability of the family, and so on. When a married couple divorces and one spouse who previously had not worked outside the home begins to work full time and the kids go to a day-care center, GDP goes up. One wonders, however, what happens to the quality of life of the children. Finally, GDP per capita tells us nothing about how the income in a nation is distributed. In many oil-rich Middle Eastern economies, the enormous wealth is concentrated in few hands. Latin American nations also have notoriously unequal income distributions. "Average" standards of living may be high even while 80 percent of the population lives in extremely poor conditions. The last two columns of Table 1.1 list income distribution statistics. The Gini index is a numerical measure that ranges from zero to 100. Higher numbers represent higher levels of income inequality. Of the countries in the table, Brazil has the worst income distribution, as represented by a Gini index of 63.4. Japan's index is the lowest at 17.0. Column seven lists the share of income that goes to the wealthiest 10 percent of households. In Brazil, over half of the nation's income is owned by the wealthiest 10 percent. As the percentage rises, income inequality worsens. Therefore, per capita income data must be used with caution. Nevertheless, we continue to refer to GDP per capita as a key measure of economic performance despite its limitations.

If the poor countries gradually caught up to the wealthy countries, economists would not have much to worry about. Growth rates in poor countries would, on average, exceed growth rates in wealthier countries until standards of living across countries were nearly equal. Every nation would end up with higher average standards of living. In fact, we do observe this to a limited extent. Japan and West Germany grew very quickly after the end of World War II. Recently South Korea, Singapore, and China, among others, grew at rates double or triple those of the wealthy industrial nations. However, the gap between many rich and poor nations continues to widen even as technology progresses and information becomes cheaper and more accessible. Why is this so? Why don't poor nations simply play "follow the leader" and imitate the successes of wealthy nations?

Perhaps some poor nations choose to remain poor. The successful transition to capitalism and the subsequent increase in economic wealth can change or destroy cultures, religions, family relationships, and communities. Some groups have much to lose in return for material gain. Many nations—Iran and China, for example—have rejected aspects of the Western capitalist economic system in part because of the cultural sacrifices that have to be made. One doubts, however, that those countries *intend* to be poor. They tried to organize economic activity differently with the hope that economic performance would also be strong. The choice to remain poor to avoid the social and cultural revolution only explains a small percentage of economic poverty.

Most nations wish to increase their material standards of living, but they either do not know how or they cannot implement the necessary changes. Economists in the past have been of limited help in giving advice. Most of the advice in the postwar era has rested on the supposition that free markets function well and that excessive government regulation is the main obstacle to growth. The advice has tended to promote privatization of government assets, deregulation, and fiscal and monetary restraint. These prescriptions are usually necessary but not sufficient to promote growth. What is left out, as I discuss extensively in this book, is that well-functioning markets require a whole set of institutions that are often missing in economies. Russia, for example, has recently privatized many assets, deregulated industries, and imposed fiscal and monetary restraint. However, its economy is on the verge of bankruptcy and collapse. Nations are extremely complex; a solution that works in one place at one time does not necessarily work in another place at another time.

The magic of compound interest highlights the importance of economic growth rates. There is a general principle called the "Rule of 69": Divide a country's GDP per capita growth rate by 69, and the result is the approximate number of years that it takes to double the country's standard of living.[1] Suppose, for example, an economy's GDP per capita grows at 1 percent per year; in this case it takes nearly 69 years, or three generations, for its citizens to be twice as well off as before. Suppose, instead, that growth rates are 2 percent per year. Now it takes only 34.5 years to double the standard of living, a generation and a half. Growth rates of 3 percent per year reduce the doubling time to about 23 years, approximately one generation. This rule shows that even a one percentage point difference in per capita growth rates makes an enormous difference over time.

As a general rule, this book advocates the position that per capita growth is good because it leads to an increase in material standards of living. It must be noted, however, that there are negative consequences to growth. For example, economic growth puts more strain on our limited resources and leads to an increase in the gas emissions that generate a greenhouse effect, which contributes to global warming. Growth also can radically change cultures, religions, and families in harmful ways. Hence the advantages of economic growth must be placed in proper perspective. This book does not focus on the harmful aspects of economic growth, but this omission does not mean that they are not important; they are simply beyond the scope of this book.

Explanations for Growth

What makes an economy's standard of living increase over time? This is perhaps the most important question that an economist can ask. A variety of answers have been given to this question. Some see education as the primary factor and point to the high levels of education attained in the developed nations. Education is much more important than it used to be given today's world of complex and rapidly changing technology. *Human capital* is the stock of knowledge that people have learned and retained. The more human capital an economy has, the more productive its labor force can be. Workers who cannot read or write are at a serious disadvantage in today's labor market. Even workers who have only a high school diploma in the United States are finding themselves shut out of many labor markets. Despite the surge in the number of college graduates in the 1970s and 1980s, the wage premium paid by employers for employees with a college degree has doubled. Education gives people skills that enable them to be more creative and more productive.

There is little doubt that education is important for economic growth. Column five of Table 1.1 lists the percentage of the selected nations' eligible population enrolled in secondary school. Many of the wealthy countries have enrollment rates in excess of 90 percent, whereas India, for example, has an enrollment rate of only 48.5 percent. However, there are three problems with viewing education as the main explanation for differences in standards of living. First, there are exceptions to the rule. Figure 1.1 plots GDP per capita against the percentage of a nation's eligible population that is enrolled in secondary school. As indicated by the solid trend line plotted in the graph, there is a positive relationship, or a

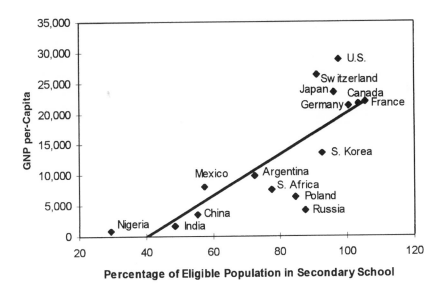

FIGURE 1.1   Education and GNP per Capita

SOURCES: *World Development Report* (New York: Oxford University Press, 1998), pp. 190–191, *World Development Report*, 1997, pp. 226–227.

positive correlation, between these variables. However, Poland, Russia, and South Korea stand out as anomalies. These countries have relatively strong educational systems, yet their levels of GNP per capita are far below those of Japan, Germany, Canada, and France.

The second problem with the education explanation lies in the issue of causality: Does education promote economic growth, or does economic growth promote education? Certainly rich nations spend greater amounts of resources on education, but perhaps this is because they can afford such spending. Advice would be easy to give if education were the answer. Nations would simply have to spend more on educating their citizens. But the problem is much more complex than that. In fact, during the 1970s many nations did increase their spending on education, but significant increases in growth did not follow.

The third problem is the contradictory empirical evidence. Mancur Olson has compared migrants from Haiti to the United States with migrants from Germany to the United States.[2] According to the 1980 U.S. Census, Haitian immigrants earned an average of $10,900 per year and those from West Germany earned an average of $21,900 per year. The wage gap is likely a result of the differences in human capital (broadly defined), so Olson assumes that someone from West Germany has on average twice the level of human capital as someone from Haiti. If human capital were the only factor explaining the difference in living standards, then Haiti should have half the per capita income of West Germany.[3] In fact, the per capita income of Haiti is at most one-tenth that of Germany. Therefore, differences in human capital explain at most one-fifth of the differences in living standards.

Another factor frequently asserted to explain differences in per capita income is a country's endowment of natural resources. The United States is blessed with numerous water streams, rich land, and abundant timber. But so are Brazil, Nigeria, and Russia. Venezuela has access to enormous oil reserves, yet its economic problems continue. Despite having few natural resources, Japanese citizens are among the wealthiest in the world. Hong Kong and Singapore, two of Asia's "Four Tigers," have achieved remarkable growth despite small land areas and almost no natural resources.[4] Natural resources make it easier for countries to grow by lowering input costs, but they can also lead to other problems. Economists Jeffrey Sachs and Andrew Warner found in a recent study that nations that had more natural resources actually had *slower* growth rates. Natural resources tended to be a curse, not a blessing.[5] They suggested that the battle over control of the natural wealth leads to corruption and bureaucratic red tape, which reduces investment and hence economic growth.

"Dutch disease" provides another example of why natural resource economies may not perform well over the long term. This phenomenon is named for the experience of the Netherlands after 1960, when large reserves of natural gas were discovered. The Dutch expected booming exports and rising prosperity. Instead the decade of the 1970s was one of rising inflation, declining manufacturing exports, lower growth rates, and rising unemployment.[6] The bad economic performance was a result of the appreciation of the Dutch currency, the guilder. Because of the large volume of natural gas exports, the demand for and hence the price of the guilder increased. The appreciation of any currency means that prices of exports increase while prices of imports decrease. Thus, the appreciation of the guilder made the Dutch economy less competitive internationally. The Dutch disease phenomenon has negative implications for a resource economy if the decrease in domestic manufacturing inhibits long-term growth. This could happen because domestic manufacturing results in learning-by-doing and aids in the transfer of technology to the domestic economy. The Dutch story can be generalized for many resource-intensive nations. Saudi Arabia, for example, produces massive oil reserves, yet its manufacturing sector is not well developed.

Perhaps the key factor in explaining economic performance is population density—the ratio of people to land area. According to this hypothesis a country with a high population density is doomed to poverty because there simply is no way to raise productivity beyond a subsistence level. Once again, however, there are too many exceptions to support this argument. Column four of Table 1.1 lists population density ratios, and Figure 1.2 plots population density against GNP per capita for

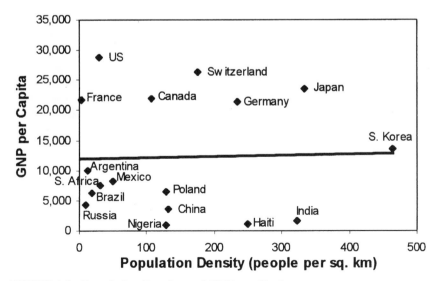

FIGURE 1.2   Population Density and GNP per Capita

SOURCE: *World Development Report* (New York: Oxford University Press, 1998), pp. 190–191.

the countries listed in Table 1.1. We would expect that, other things being equal, higher population density would tend to lower GNP per capita. The trend line plotted in Figure 1.2 should have a negative slope. In fact, however, the trend line shows essentially no slope. The paradoxes abound. Japan has a high population density *and* a high GNP per capita. The country with the highest population density is Hong Kong, yet Hong Kong has the fourth highest per capita income of all the countries listed.[7] Many of the poorest countries, such as Brazil, Russia, and even China, have population densities lower than those of Switzerland and Germany. These two countries have per capita incomes ten times as high as those of the poorest countries. Clearly other factors are driving differences in living standards.

A fourth possibility for explaining differences in living standards across nations is technology. Here the hypothesis would be that countries are wealthy because they have access to technology, which makes workers very productive. Mainstream economics, in particular neoclassical growth theory (which we examine in Chapter 2), certainly validates this assertion both theoretically and empirically. However, this answer does not get to the root of the problem. We can rephrase the question this way: Why do some nations have advanced technology but others do not? Most technology is freely available. Much of the remainder can be bought. Payments from developing countries for technology are often estimated to be less than one one-thousandth of GDP.[8] Why don't all nations use the most up-to-date technology? Why don't all nations produce advanced technology? Chapter 5 elaborates on this set of questions.

Perhaps some nations decades and centuries ago could grow because they were the "pioneers" of growth and there was not a developed world then to inhibit their growth. International markets were not already cluttered with enormous amounts of goods, and the first countries could grow without worrying about competition and political obstacles from existing countries. This is the essence of dependency theory, which asserts that the wealthy developed nations trap the poor nations into a cycle of poverty. We return to dependency theory in detail in Chapter 2.

The preceding discussion is not meant to be exhaustive but rather to list a few of the more common explanations for disparities in per capita income. The central hypothesis of this book is that a nation's institutional framework is the key to unlocking its wealth potential. In a static sense, institutions define the costs of transacting and the ability of organizations to capture the gains from specialization and division of labor. In a dynamic sense, institutions define the incentive structure under which organizations operate and determine whether or not organizations undertake activities that advance technology. A nation that grows over time does so because its institutions encourage and promote that growth. A nation stagnates over time because its institutions encourage economic stagnation. This is not a new idea; economists have made this assertion before. But the idea is just beginning to gain wide acceptance. It faced much resistance in the past, because traditional economic theory had no role for institutions; they were implicit in the analysis. Because of the work of Ronald Coase, which is described in Chapter 3, institutions can now be integrated directly into economic theory. We will pursue this argument throughout the book.

The focus of "development" in this book is per capita income. We are not directly concerned with the distribution of income, although, as noted earlier, this is clearly as important as growth. We know from economic history, however, that a high level of per capita income and a reasonably fair income distribution can coexist. As nations become wealthier, they can create institutions to better share the wealth. One thing is certain: If the pie does not grow, one person can have a bigger slice only by taking it from another. For our purposes, then, good economic performance is defined as rapid growth in per capita income. We do not explicitly model the income distribution systems.

Institutions and Organizations

The word "institution" has a variety of meanings in the English language. To avoid confusion, only one of its meanings is employed here. *Institutions* are the "rules of the game" in a society. They are the rules that society establishes for human interaction. Institutions reduce the uncertainty involved in human interaction by giving us patterns for our behavior.[9] Because of the set of institutions we have, most daily interaction is routine. We know how to greet one another on the streets, we know how we are supposed to act in social settings, we know what is acceptable behavior and what is not, we know what time we are supposed to eat lunch and dinner, and so on. The institutional framework has three components: formal rules, informal rules, and enforcement mechanisms.

Formal rules are the written rules of society. Laws governing contracts, crime, political systems, product information, the imposition of tariffs or quotas, taxes, the regulation of banks, and so on are all formal institutions. Typically the constitution is the ultimate formal institution of a nation; all of the nation's laws must comply with this document. Formal rules can be created by firms as well as governments. For example, a university has a whole set of formal institutions. In order to graduate, students must successfully complete a minimum number of credit hours while fulfilling requirements in general education and in a major field of study. There is a minimum number of hours during which faculty must meet with students (contact hours), and there is a grading system to evaluate individual performance. All of these are part of the university's institutions. Note that in this usage the university itself is *not* an institution. We refer to universities and other entities as *organizations*. The distinction is subtle but crucial. Organizations are discussed later.

Informal rules are the unwritten rules of society. These include culture, norms of behavior, codes of conduct, and so on. Citizens of a country grow up learning all kinds of unwritten norms and attitudes. In some cultures, families are the central social unit. This is not something that is written into formal law. The attitude toward women and the acceptable roles for men and women differ across nations. Meal times are often set by custom. Informal rules tell us what to wear to certain events. For example, people in the United States tend to dress very casually compared to those in Latin America and Europe. The informal rules of a nation can be so ingrained that people are not aware of them. But anyone who visits another nation quickly notices some of these cultural differences.

The third component of the institutional framework is *enforcement*. Institutions often are ineffective if they are not enforced. For example, a nation can have antitrust laws that prevent firms from becoming monopolies, but if the government does not enforce such laws, businesses may act as if the antitrust laws did not exist. Some institutions are self-enforcing. People in the United States drive on the right side of the road even when no police officer is in sight. To do otherwise is to take your life into your own hands. Students seldom cheat on examinations when the professor leaves the room, because the ethics that they were taught as children matter. Enforcement is not an all-or-nothing phenomenon. Countries may enforce laws vigorously, marginally, or not at all. Enforcement is an integral part of a nation's institutional framework and, as we shall see, may be the single most important element in explaining differences in economic performance.

Institutions can be economic, political, or social in nature. Tax laws are generally economic institutions, though they have social elements as well, especially in regards to income distribution. Laws that govern the election of presidents or prime ministers are political institutions. Laws that create and govern welfare programs and crime and punishment are social institutions. All these types of institutions are important. In fact, a country's political institutions often dictate how other institutions are created. The U.S. Constitution, for example, delegates the ability to create formal institutions to the Congress.

Organizations are groups of individuals bound together to achieve some objective. Examples of organizations are corporations, small businesses, the Congress, the Supreme Court, families, political parties, sports teams, and so on. The term is purposely kept general. The important point is to distinguish organizations from institutions. Two examples clarify the distinction.

Major League Baseball is an organization. This organization creates the institutional framework that baseball teams (organizations) such as the St. Louis Cardinals and the New York Yankees follow. Baseball has a number of formal institutions: Teams play nine innings to complete a game; there are nine players allowed on the field; a player must use a wooden bat; a ball caught before it hits the ground is an "out"; each team has three outs per inning; and so on. Baseball also has informal institutions: The pitcher should not purposefully try to injure batters; rookies do not give advice to veterans; a player tips his hat after making a spectacular play; and so on. Finally, enforcement is carried out by four umpires.

Microsoft is an organization. Its goal is to maximize profits by creating software for consumers. It operates under an institutional framework. For example, Microsoft cannot "bundle" its applications software with its Windows operating system, and it must pay income taxes. There are nondiscrimination rules that Microsoft must follow when hiring and firing workers. The organization must publicly disclose its assets and liabilities. The company cannot export its products to certain countries without an explicit exemption from the federal government. The list goes on.

Organizations can also create their own institutions. Wells Fargo Bank can impose a dress code on its employees and require them to work certain hours. There may be a bonus system to provide added incentives.

It is critical that the distinction between institutions and organizations be clear for a proper understanding of what follows in this book. Institutions are the rules, the regulations, and the enforcement mechanisms. Organizations are groups bound together to achieve an objective.

A Road Map

Where do we go from here? The next chapter discusses traditional theories of growth. We examine and critique dependency theory and neoclassical growth theory, two important possibilities for explaining economic performance. Chapter 3 discusses the concept of transaction costs and provides the theoretical link to institutions. Chapters 4 and 5 explain the impact of institutions on economies in both a static and a dynamic sense. Chapter 6 examines various political systems that produce the formal institutions. Chapter 7 elaborates on specific theoretical issues that transition economies face, and Chapter 8 applies the theory of institutions to Poland and Russia. Chapter 9 discusses the issues confronting developing economies. Chapter 10 applies the theory of institutions to the developing economies of Mexico and South Korea. Finally, Chapter 11 focuses on a case study of China and the recent reversion of Hong Kong from a British colony to a Chinese republic.

Questions for Discussion

1. List three possible explanations for disparities in living standards besides those mentioned in this chapter. Which of the three do you consider to be the most important? Why?
2. Define institutions and organizations. Give an example of each.
3. Think of your favorite sport. Identify three institutions and three organizations affiliated with the sport.

Notes

1. The "Rule of 69" is derived from the formula $P_t = P_0 e^{rt}$, which in log form solving for t reduces to $t = (\ln P_t - \ln P_0)/r$. Setting $P_t = 2$ and $P_0 = 1$ yields $t = \ln (2) / r$.

2. Mancur Olson, "Big Bills Left on the Sidewalk: Why Some Nations Are Rich, and Others Poor," *Journal of Economic Perspectives*, vol. 10 (2) (Spring 1996), p. 18.

3. One criticism of this assumption is that some of the wage gap is driven by racial discrimination. If the Haitian wages were adjusted for discrimination, then the wage gap would decrease. But any factor that *narrows* the wage gap between Haitian and German immigrants only reinforces the claim that differences in human capital explain a small portion of the differences in living standards, since the per capita income gap between Haiti and Germany is so large.

4. The "Four Tigers" are the countries of Singapore and South Korea and the Chinese provinces of Hong Kong and Taiwan. Hong Kong officially became part of China on July 1, 1997, and many governments around the world consider Taiwan to be quasi-independent.

5. Peter Passel, "Economic Scene: The Curse of Natural Resources," *New York Times*, September 21, 1995, and Jeffrey D. Sachs and Andrew M. Warner, "Natural Resource Abundance and Economic Growth," National Bureau of Economic Research (NBER) Working Paper No. 5398, December 1995.

6. Malcolm Gillis, Dwight H. Perkins, Michael Roemer, and Donald S. Snodgrass, *Economics of Development* (New York: W. W. Norton, 1992), p. 434.

7. Hong Kong is not plotted in the graph to maintain scaling for the other countries.

8. Olson, "Big Bills Left on the Sidewalk," p. 8.

9. Douglass C. North, *Institutions, Institutional Change, and Economic Performance* (New York: Cambridge University Press, 1990).

2

Dependency Theory and Neoclassical Growth Theory

Various scholars have tried to explain the great disparity in living standards across countries. Here we focus on two strands of this vast literature: dependency theory as it was elaborated by the Economic Commission for Latin America (ECLA), and neoclassical growth theory. The ECLA, a UN regional body, was highly influential in the post–World War II era, especially in Latin America, though its influence has diminished considerably since the early 1980s. Neoclassical growth theory has received more attention from economists in the 1980s and 1990s. It is well accepted in mainstream economic theory.

Dependency Theory

In its simplest form, dependency theory argues that poor countries are poor because rich countries are rich. A dependency theorist views the world economies as composed of two distinct groups, the core and the periphery. The *core* consists of the wealthy, developed nations that produce the technologically advanced manufactured goods. The *periphery* consists of the remaining poorer, developing countries that produce and export raw materials. The dependency school is an advanced body of thought that has branched in many directions. This section is not a survey of the literature; the focus here is on one strand of the literature that has had important influences on economic thought.

A sophisticated version of dependency theory was first drafted in 1948 by Raúl Prebisch, head of the ECLA.[1] The conventional economic wisdom at the time was that the periphery enjoyed the benefits of the core's development and industrialization through international trade. Therefore, there was no need for the periphery to industrialize. As productivity increased in the core, the prices of manufactured goods fell and the *terms of trade* in the periphery improved. The terms of trade is defined as the ratio of imports to exports or, equivalently, the price of exports divided by the price of imports. If the terms of trade improve, a nation can purchase more imports for a given amount of exports, and the average standard of living in the country increases. Therefore, international trade makes everyone better off—even the periphery nations, which continue to concentrate on raw-materials production.

Prebisch and the ECLA argued that this conventional wisdom was wrong because the gains from the industrialization in the core failed to benefit the periphery in a significant way. Even if both the core and the periphery were made better off, the vast majority of the gains went to the core. Hence the gains from trade were unequal at best. The productivity gains resulted in higher wages, higher profits, and shorter working hours in the core countries while leaving the periphery virtually unaffected.

Moreover, Prebisch provided evidence that, in fact, the terms of trade worsened in Latin America between the 1870s and the 1930s. The prices of Latin America's imports from the core rose faster than the prices of Latin American exports. The situation was likely to deteriorate further in the future, as import demand for capital, technology, and consumer goods increased in the periphery, putting constant pressure on the trade balance. The solution was for the periphery to industrialize. The foreign exchange earnings from raw-materials exports had to be channeled into capital equipment for new industries, a policy known as *import substitution industrialization* (ISI). The goal of ISI was to develop a domestic manufacturing sector that would produce the previously imported goods.

The argument advanced by the ECLA was a powerful one, and it greatly influenced Latin American policy over the next few decades. If the core was to blame for the cycle of poverty in the periphery by slowing or blocking the process of industrialization, then the cycle had to be broken by forced industrialization of the periphery.

Is the ECLA argument valid? Despite significant advances, nearly forty years after the publication of the ECLA report and four decades of ISI, Latin America remains an underdeveloped region. There is no doubt that living standards have improved, in some cases considerably. Yet even in the wealthiest nations in Latin America—in Argentina, Chile, and Brazil, for example—living standards are one-fourth the level of those in the United States, as measured by GDP per capita.

Dependency theory highlights a central truth of many developing countries. Some periphery countries are very dependent on wealthy nations for a significant portion of aggregate demand and for advanced intermediate inputs into production. Periphery countries earn vital foreign exchange by exporting to the core. Table 2.1 shows the ratio of exports to GDP for various nations. Other things being equal, the larger this ratio or percentage, the more important is the export sector. When Ecuador goes

TABLE 2.1   Importance of Exports

Country	Exports as a Percent of 1997 GDP
Brazil	6
Argentina	9
Japan	9
United States	11
India	12
China	20
France	23
Germany	24
Poland	26
Ecuador	32
S. Korea	38
Canada	38

SOURCE: *World Development Report* (New York: Oxford University Press, 1998), pp. 214–215.

into a recession, for example, the United States barely notices, because such a small fraction of U.S. production goes to Ecuador. However, the reverse is not true. When the United States enters a recession, big shock waves are transmitted to Ecuador via a fall in demand for Ecuador's exports. However, the data in Table 2.1 call into question the export dependency of many periphery nations. There are many developing countries, such as Argentina and Brazil, that have a small ratio of exports to GDP, and many wealthy countries, such as Canada and France, that have high ratios. Argentina, for example, does not seem any more dependent on exports to fuel its economy than the United States, yet its economic performance has been relatively poor in the postwar era.

Periphery countries are dependent on the core in that they must rely on imported capital equipment and the technology embedded in that capital for necessary inputs into industrial production. This remains so even after decades of ISI policies. ISI did not lessen the dependence of the periphery on the core but altered the form of the dependence from consumer goods to intermediate inputs. One must question why the periphery has not been able to develop the necessary technology to produce the capital inputs on its own.

Even if one accepts the fact that developing nations are to a large extent dependent on the core, does this dependency mean that the core traps the periphery into a cycle of poverty? Dependency theory argues that the answer is yes and that the cycle must be broken. An extreme policy response is to drastically reduce trade with the core by imposing protectionist barriers. This has the effect of severely depressing the export sectors in the periphery, which causes a recession or depression in the short term. The country is left with lower profits for domestic investment and less foreign exchange for the importation of capital and other goods. Moreover, domestic consumption must fall with the decline of imports. However, since the cycle of poverty is to be broken with the disruption of trade, dependency theory suggests that the recession is temporary and that domestically generated growth follows.

The ECLA did not advocate such an extreme position. All that was needed was to convert the profits from the export sectors into capital for industrialization. The export sector should not be sacrificed for industrialization to occur. The ECLA recommended that the periphery find a balance between export production and industrialization.

Though this is a powerful and persuasive argument, there are several weaknesses to dependency theory. First, there is no convincing evidence of a long-term decline in the terms of trade for the periphery. Terms of trade have indeed declined in some periods for some countries. But terms of trade rely heavily on the prices of primary commodities, particularly oil. When oil prices were high in the 1970s, the terms of trade rose significantly in some periphery countries. Since periphery countries' exports are less diversified, they are more likely to be subject to large and sudden shifts in the terms of trade. But there is no evidence to indicate a persistent decline in the terms of trade over time.

Second, the ties between the core and the periphery are exaggerated in dependency theory. Many core nations, including the United States, are highly self-sufficient, and no matter how important the export sector is to certain periphery countries, the domestic sector is much more important. Net exports are typically a small portion of GDP, swamped by domestic consumption and investment. If links from the core to the periphery are the main forces of underdevelopment in the periphery, one would expect strong trade ties between the two groups. But most trade of the core economies is with other core economies, not with the periphery.

Third, the concept of dividing the world in two distinct arenas, the core and periphery, seems too simplistic. The world's largest producer of primary products is the United States. Many "periphery" nations have large manufacturing sectors, especially after thirty or more years of ISI. Even if the distinction between core and periphery was useful twenty or thirty years ago, it is less so today.

The fourth weakness is the accumulating empirical evidence that there is a *positive* correlation between "dependency" as measured by reliance on the trade and export sector and economic growth. Many of the Asian countries, such as Taiwan and Korea and, before them, Japan, have seemingly broken from the grip of the core and even joined the core, not by isolating themselves but by pursuing aggressive export policies. At the same time, Latin America experimented with three decades of import substitution policies, raising tariff barriers and importing large quantities of capital for industrialization. Some gains were made, but relatively speaking, Latin America fell further behind the Asian economies. These examples from both Asia and Latin America contradict the policy prescriptions of dependency theory.

Finally, dependency theory blames outside forces, the core, for lack of development. There is no internal critical reflection and no domestic policy prescription for reform. Dependency theory seems to deny the periphery autonomy in the world order, locating blame on the outside instead of looking for internal factors that might be to blame. For example, the ECLA version of dependency theory failed to explain why the process of industrialization was not occurring naturally in Latin America. Could the profits from the export sector have been channeled into productive domestic investment without the need for import substitution? What was the *internal* reason that this process was not occurring? Dependency theory discourages such questioning. Without critical reflection, there is no movement for change or reform in the developing countries themselves.

What are we to make of all this? Dependency theory forcefully draws out some truths about economic relationships between developed and developing economies. The ECLA provided a convincing theory of how the core nations trap the periphery into a cycle of poverty that must be broken with forced industrialization. But is the theory correct? Perhaps industrialization did need to occur in the developing countries, but for reasons different from those the ECLA suggested. There may be a natural limit to growth fueled solely by the export sector, especially one that produces raw materials. For instance, resources in a country could diminish, which would dampen export production. Perhaps with increasing labor productivity in the export sector but slow growth in demand for the export products, demand for labor would decrease. Without other alternatives, the labor would have nowhere to turn for new employment and unemployment would continually increase. These alternative reasons for why nations need to industrialize have nothing to do with the relationship between the core and the periphery. Nor do these alternative explanations suggest the adoption of import substitution policies; industrialization with an outward orientation would have been preferable. So the ECLA's prescription of industrialization may have been correct, but for the wrong reasons. If so, the call for ISI was misguided and actually hindered growth in Latin America. In the final analysis, dependency theory offers little insight to what reforms are necessary in the developing countries themselves. We must look elsewhere for answers.

Neoclassical Growth Theory

Neoclassical growth theory grew out of work done by Robert Solow in the late 1950s. It is a macroeconomic approach to dynamic growth. The most basic concept is that an economy's output is represented by an aggregate production function of the form $Y = F(K,L)$ where Y represents real output (GDP), K is the nation's capital stock, L is labor, and $F(.)$ is a functional form representing the technology that transforms the capital and labor inputs into output. In other words, output is the result of capital and labor inputs combined with a level of technology. Capital is defined in this sense as all nonlabor inputs into the production process—machinery, buildings, land, computers, and even education (part of human capital).

Neoclassical growth theory assumes that the production function exhibits *constant returns to scale*. This means that a doubling of capital and labor inputs results in a doubling of output. This assumption does two things. First, it implies that the size of an economy has no separate effect on growth. Small countries can grow just as easily as large countries. Second, it allows us to express output as a function of capital per worker. Dividing the production function by Y, we obtain $y = f(k)$, where y is output per worker (Y/L), and k is capital per worker (K/L). Per capita output, then, depends solely on the stock of capital per worker.[2]

An example will serve to illustrate the point. Two nations, Japan and Korea, have access to the same technology, but Japan has a higher level of per capita output than Korea. According to neoclassical growth theory, the only reason for this higher output is that Japanese workers have access to more machines, tools, and other equipment to make them more productive. Imagine two secretaries. One has access to a telephone, computer, printer, fax machine, and adding machine. The other has only a telephone and a manual typewriter. The first secretary is far more productive, because he or she can accomplish more things with the given capital stock. Similarly, if construction workers have access to expensive machinery to dig ditches, surface roads, and so on, they will be far more productive than construction workers who work with shovels. The ratio of capital per worker determines the nation's standard of living.

The per-worker production function exhibits *diminishing returns to scale*. That is, as the capital-to-labor ratio rises, output per worker increases, but at a decreasing rate. Suppose the secretary with just a telephone and manual typewriter acquires a computer and a printer. Productivity goes up significantly (once the secretary becomes proficient at using the computer). If the same secretary then acquires a second computer, productivity may go up slightly, but certainly by less than the increase from the first computer. Most of what can be accomplished with two computers can be accomplished with just one computer. Suppose the secretary acquires a third computer. Chances are that this computer will sit untouched and will only be used in rare circumstances. The increase in output of the secretary attributable to the acquisition of the third computer is far below the increase in output from the first computer. In other words, as the capital-to-labor ratio rises, output continues to rise, but at a slower rate. Eventually, the additional capital adds practically nothing to output. In economic terminology, we say that *the marginal product* of the capital approaches zero. The per-worker production function is represented in Figure 2.1. Capital per worker (k) is plotted on the horizontal axis, and output per worker (y) on the vertical axis. The production function constantly increases, but at a decreasing rate. The slope represents the concept of diminishing returns.

Why is it that the aggregate production function has constant returns to scale, whereas the per-worker production function exhibits diminishing marginal returns? Part of the answer is that the production functions behave this way because we assume that to be the case. But there is more. The concept of *returns to scale* implies that *all* inputs must increase in the same proportion. Labor must increase exactly in proportion to the capital stock. In contrast, the per-worker production function assumes that the capital stock is growing more rapidly than the labor force. Therefore, not all inputs are increasing in the same proportion, and the principle of returns to scale does not apply. Instead, the principle of diminishing returns sets in. The *law of diminishing marginal returns* states that if more and more of an input is used, holding all other inputs constant, eventually the additional output (or the marginal product) will decrease. Using our secretary example, the returns-to-scale principle requires that labor (hours worked) and capital (computers) increase in the same proportion. But if only capital increases with no corresponding increase in labor hours, then diminishing returns sets in. Thus diminishing returns to capital is consistent with basic economic theory even in the context of a constant returns-to-scale production function.

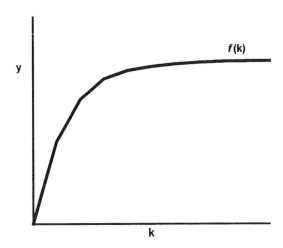

FIGURE 2.1   The Per-Worker Production Function

The per-worker production function determines the relationship between the capital stock per worker and output per worker, but it does not determine the equilibrium level of capital per worker (and hence the level of output per worker) that the economy will achieve. To explain this, we need to understand the forces that create and destroy capital. *Investment*, in the economic sense of the word, is the purchase of a newly produced asset that expands the productive capacity of the economy. In other words, it is the purchase of something that is used to produce something else. A farm tractor is a classic example of investment. Farmers purchase tractors in order to produce food. Likewise, businesses purchase computers to help them produce their products more efficiently. Investment adds to the stock of capital. With certain simplifying assumptions, we know that a nation's level of saving equals its level of investment.[3] If we take the saving rate, s, to be a fixed percentage of output per worker, then investment in an economy is equal to s • f(k). The resulting investment curve is plotted in Figure 2.2.

At the same time, part of the capital stock wears out each year. This is called *depreciation*. It is reasonable to assume that a certain percentage of the capital stock wears out each year or, equivalently, that a certain percentage of the capital stock per worker wears out each year. We represent the rate of depreciation by the symbol δ; hence total depreciation in the economy is δk. As the capital stock per worker rises, so does the level of depreciation. Figure 2.3 demonstrates this depreciation line.

The *steady state* is a dynamic equilibrium position in which output per worker does not change from one year to the next. In other words, the standard of living reaches a certain level and remains there. An economy

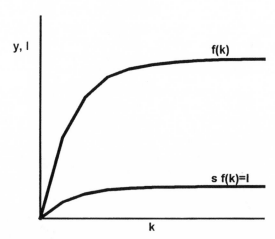

FIGURE 2.2   The Saving Function

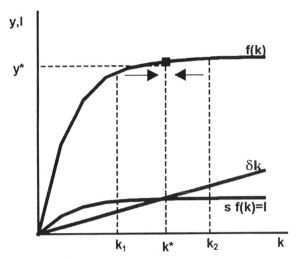

FIGURE 2.3   Saving and Depreciation

settles at a steady state when capital per worker does not change, or when the forces that create capital per worker are equal to the forces that destroy capital per worker. Such a situation occurs in Figure 2.3 where the investment line crosses the depreciation line at k*. The capital stock per worker in this economy is k* and, following k* up to the production function, the level of output per worker is y*.

What would happen if the economy were at a point like k_1? Since investment exceeds depreciation at k_1, capital per worker and hence output per worker would increase. The capital creation continues until the economy reaches k*. Consequently, output per worker rises until the economy reaches y*. If the economy is at a point like k_2, depreciation exceeds investment and the capital stock per worker declines until the economy reaches k* and y*. Note that the steady-state level of output per worker is determined by two forces: the rate of saving, s, and the rate of depreciation, δ. The higher the rate of saving, the larger is the steady-state level of output per worker. Conversely, the higher the rate of depreciation, the lower the level of output per worker. A key policy prescription from neoclassical growth theory, then, is to increase saving rates in developing countries, which will increase the capital-to-labor ratio and standards of living.

The main conclusion from neoclassical growth theory, however, is a bit surprising. Even if saving rates are increased, the rate of investment increases, leading to an increase in capital per worker. Eventually, however, the rate of depreciation equals the rate of investment, and the economy's standard of living stops rising. So an increase in saving rates only leads to a temporary boost in output per worker. *In the long run, the level of saving has no effect at all on living standards.* The only force that leads to sustained and continuous increases in living standards is one that continually shifts the per-worker production function upward. That force is technology. An economy must have continuous technological advancements in order to continue growing over time. Assuming that nations can imitate other nations' technologies easily (which is a big assumption), one or a few nations can lead the way in technological advancements, and other nations can follow along. Figure 2.4 models the impact of technology. Since technology makes capital more productive, a given stock of capital per worker produces more output. Therefore, the entire per worker production function shifts upward. The ratio of capital per worker k* now produces output level y' instead of the lower level of y*.

Neoclassical growth theory is very appealing because it manages to describe the complex process of economic growth using simple equations and concepts. It clearly shows that short-run growth results from higher rates of saving, whereas long-run growth depends on advances in technology. We know from this model that the key to the long-run success of an economy lies in its ability either to create or to imitate technology. We return to this central role of technology in Chapter 5.

Neoclassical growth theory suffers from two serious weaknesses, however. The first is that it predicts a fairly rapid *convergence* of levels of wealth across nations. Recall that diminishing returns to capital mean that the marginal productivity of that capital decreases as the capital stock grows. Thus one dollar of capital invested in a country such as India with a low capital-to-labor ratio should have a much greater impact

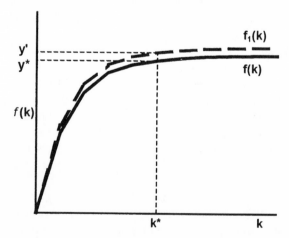

FIGURE 2.4   Technology and the Per-Worker Production Function

on output than a dollar of capital invested in the United States, where capital-to-labor ratios are already high. Thus one of the implications from the theory is that given approximately equal saving rates, poor countries should grow faster than wealthy countries.[4] Standards of living across borders should converge. In fact, using realistic estimates of aggregate production functions, convergence should occur in a relatively short period of time. However, we do not observe this convergence in the real world.[5] In fact, the gap between many rich and poor countries is increasing. Moreover, patterns of investment in the world indicate that rates of return in the United States are comparable to or higher than rates of return in many developing countries. This also contradicts what we would expect from the theory, since poor countries should have high marginal productivities of capital. The theory of institutions discussed in this book does not predict convergence. Countries can persist in relative poverty for decades or perhaps centuries.

The second weakness of neoclassical growth theory is that at best the theory seems to *describe* growth but does not explain it. The main conclusion is that technology drives increases in living standards in the long run, yet the theory has nothing to say about what makes technology levels increase. It may lead us in the right direction, but it leaves the main mystery unsolved. Technology is completely *exogenous* in this model—that is, the level of technology is determined outside the model.[6] The theory of institutions does not necessarily contradict neoclassical growth theory, but it goes beyond description and examines the underlying causes of economic growth and stagnation.

Questions for Discussion

1. If the ratio of a country's imports to exports rises, what happens to its terms of trade?
2. Do you think it is useful to divide the economies of the world into the core and the periphery? Why or why not?
3. Name three criticisms of dependency theory.
4. Suppose Country A has a higher population growth rate than Country B, but both countries have the same saving rate, the same level of technology, and the same depreciation rate. Which country will have the higher steady-state level of per capita output? Why?
5. What is the difference between "diminishing returns to scale" and "diminishing marginal returns?"
6. Despite the shortcomings of dependency theory and neoclassical growth theory, are they useful? Why or why not?

Notes

1. United Nations, Economic Commission for Latin America, "The Economic Development of Latin America and Its Principal Problems" (New York: United Nations Department of Economic Affairs, 1950).

2. The full result is $y = f(k, L/L) = f(k,1)$. However, a functional transformation of a constant is economically irrelevant. Therefore, we can ignore the constant, and the term collapses to $y = f(k)$.

3. This identity assumes that the government's budget is perfectly balanced and that there is no trade imbalance with other nations. The more complex identity states that saving is equal to investment plus the government budget deficit plus net exports. Government deficits are the nation's "dissaving," and a trade surplus results in net capital outflows.

4. Another assumption required for convergence is that population growth rates across countries are equal. A high rate of population growth means that the existing capital stock must be spread over more people, lowering the steady-state level of capital per worker. I have left this out of the model to simplify the analysis.

5. There is a vast literature in economics called the New Growth Theory that tries to remedy this weakness by getting rid of the assumption of diminishing returns to capital. Without diminishing returns, poor nations are not expected to grow more quickly than wealthy nations, and convergence is not a necessary eventuality.

6. Again, New Growth Theory attempts to correct this weakness by making technology endogenous—determined within the model.

3

The Coase Theorem: The Link to Institutions

Economic Efficiency

Traditional neoclassical economic theory preaches the virtues of the *efficient* outcome. Efficiency in economics has a precise meaning. It means that all mutual gains from trade have been exhausted. There is no trade opportunity left that would make someone better off without hurting someone else. The concept of efficiency is ultimately derived from the philosophy of utilitarianism, whose guiding principle is the greatest good for the greatest number. If there is a potential trade that results in a net gain to society, then the trade should be undertaken; the only proviso is that it not make anyone worse off. In other words, efficiency does not imply that the poor steal from the rich even though there might be a net gain to society from doing so, because the rich will be made worse off.

Economic theory (particularly microeconomic theory) is centered on the concept of efficiency. Students in introductory microeconomic courses are taught, for example, that the efficient outcome is a world of perfect competition in which all firms earn the normal rate of return on their operations. This is efficient because all possible trades between buyer and seller have been exhausted.[1] In fact, the entire build-up of neoclassical microeconomic theory leads to the "invisible hand" doctrine first stated by Adam Smith more than 200 years ago.

[B]y directing that industry in such a manner as its produce may be of the greatest value, he intends only his own gain, and he is in this, as in many other cases, led by an invisible hand to promote an end which was no part of his intention. Nor is it always the worse for the society that it was no part of it. By pursuing his own interest he frequently promotes that of the society more effectually than when he really intends to promote it. I have never known much good done by those who affected to trade for the public good.[2]

This doctrine states that the social welfare of a nation is maximized *precisely because* each person acts in his or her self-interest. To put it bluntly, individuals produce the best possible economic world, the efficient world, by focusing first on their own needs and desires. How can this be? Consumers have limited budgets yet unlimited wants and needs. In this context, the best thing that consumers can do is to purchase the goods and services that they most desire. Producers, on the other hand, seek to maximize profits. They do this by producing the goods and services that consumers want the most. As long as there is free entry and exit into industries and good information about products, the desire for profits will generate competition that lowers the price charged to consumers. With a few other assumptions, perfect competition and economic efficiency appear. This theory leads to a policy prescription of *laissez-faire*, or hands off. Governments should let markets operate with little regulation. The "invisible hand" will take over and lead to the production and exchange that are necessary to tap the wealth potential of the economy.

Underlying the discussion thus far has been an assumption that is so subtle that the economics profession did not even notice it until the work of Ronald Coase. Yet when the implications of relaxing this assumption are thought through, the inability of neoclassical economics to explain many real-world events becomes clearer. The assumption is this: *Neoclassical economic theory assumes that the process of exchange is costless.* In other words, all exchanges are made in the context of good information with no possibility of one party's not honoring the agreement. This assumption rarely holds in the real world, however. An example can serve to illustrate the point.

Rachel is a brilliant college graduate who needs financing to start up her new computer software business. She is developing software that allows firms to track their inventory at a lower cost than existing software. However, she needs funds to purchase expensive diagnostic hardware and then to market her product. Rachel has developed a business plan, and early results show that her software will be popular. The bankers, however, are unwilling to lend her the funds because she is young and inexperienced, and she has no collateral to guarantee a loan. Furthermore, the bankers are not experts in the computer industry, and they do not know whether her product will be completed in a timely manner or whether the product will sell well. The financing does not come through, and Rachel is forced to abandon her software production. Note that the transaction between Rachel and the bank would have been beneficial for both parties and for the economy as a whole, but the transaction did not take place.

Transaction Costs

In this example, trade did not occur because of the high transaction costs. *Transaction costs* are the costs of negotiating, measuring, and enforcing exchanges. Negotiating an agreement can be a long and costly process. All sides to the exchange must bargain with one another even when they are in bitter opposition. Labor unions and management must negotiate new contracts periodically. Sometimes the process is so difficult that mediators must be brought in to facilitate the discussions. The 1994–1995 Major League Baseball strike cost millions of dollars to both sides. Clearly the stoppage of play was harmful to the players, the owners, and the fans. According to Coase, "In order to carry out a market transaction, it is necessary to discover who it is that one wishes to deal with, to inform people that one wishes to deal and on what terms, to conduct negotiations leading up to a bargain, to draw up the contract. . . . "[3] These are all elements in negotiating an exchange. In our software example, negotiating costs were small but not zero.

Measurement costs involve measuring all the attributes of a good or service. The root source of measurement costs is poor information. For example, when purchasing a computer, the buyer would like to know a lot more about the computer's attributes than simply the price. How fast does it run the software? Will it last for a reasonable period of time? It is upgradable? Measurement problems abound in the purchase of a used car. Is the car reliable? How sound is the engine? Will the body rust over time? Measurement costs are often worse for services than for goods. How do we know how good a doctor is when trying to select one? When a corporation hires a law firm to defend a lawsuit, it must ascertain the quality of the representation it will get. In our software example, the bank faced high measurement costs because it could not perfectly ascertain Rachel's skill level as a programmer, nor could it know the market conditions and the true potential of the software. In the absence of collateral, the bank decided that the loan was too risky.

There are some measures that can be taken to lower measurement costs. One is to provide a seller's warranty guaranteeing the quality of the product for a particular time. A used car salesman, for example, could offer a money-back guarantee that the car will function properly for at least one year. Another way to lower measurement costs is to deal only with friends or relatives, or to make decisions on the basis of recommendations from others. For example, many people select a doctor on the basis of experiences that their friends have had. The same is true for lawyers. Reputation is also important. If the word gets out that a particular law firm is not very strong, then potential clients shy away. Measurement costs can be reduced, but they can rarely be eliminated.

Finally, transaction costs include the costs of enforcing exchanges. Differences in enforcement costs across countries may be the single most important reason why some nations are wealthy and others are poor. Once an agreement is reached, the parties to the agreement must honor their commitments. But there is always the chance that the other party will not do so. If there is no enforcement mechanism to penalize and deter contract breakers, then either side to an agreement can achieve short-term gains by not fulfilling its part of agreement. For example, suppose that a construction firm contracts with a real estate firm to build new houses in a subdivision. The real estate agency pays the firm as it completes the houses, only to discover two years later that the construction firm used inferior materials and the houses have serious defects that need to be repaired. If the real estate firm has no recourse to sue or otherwise recover its expenses from the contractor, then it must absorb the entire expense for the repair or place the burden on the homeowners. Lack of enforcement makes the exchange much riskier. In the software example, Rachel could not convince the bank that she would honor her part of the agreement. Indeed, Rachel herself did not know for sure that her product would be successful. Because of the bank's lack of ability to enforce the agreement, it refused the loan.

Reputation, repeat dealings, and competition help to lower enforcement costs. If a firm is concerned with its name recognition, then it may honor agreements in order to sustain its good public relations image. If a customer and business are engaged in repeated exchange over time, then both sides also have an incentive to honor their agreements. If I routinely go to a particular bicycle store to purchase bike accessories and have repairs done, then I do not want to harm that relationship by knowingly writing a bad check. On the other hand, the owner of the bike store has an incentive to treat me fairly, because he knows that I can take my business elsewhere. Underlying the self-enforcing characteristics of reputation and repeat exchanges is an assumption that there is competition in the marketplace. If the bike store is the only one in town, then I may have to live with low-quality service if I want my bicycle maintained. Thus the power of competition is key to enforcing exchanges.

In many nations, however, competition is sparse. And in many markets, customers and suppliers are not engaged in repeat dealings. Moreover, even when these factors are present, many exchanges are so large or so complicated that there are gray areas in the contract. A recent example is a contract between the U.S. government and computer programmers to develop a new computer system to handle Medicare billing.[4] The programmers began work on the system, only to discover that the process was far more complex, and hence would take much more time, than initially thought. Because of substantial cost overruns, the government canceled the contract. Was this a case of the government's not fulfilling its side of the exchange? More likely the root problem in this transaction was the inability to properly measure all the attributes of the exchange. If negotiation, measurement, or enforcement costs are high, then transaction costs are high, and many potential exchanges will be forfeited.

The Coase Theorem

In 1960 Ronald Coase published an article that clarified the role of trans-action costs in neoclassical economic theory.[5] His finding has come to be called the *Coase theorem*. The theorem states that in a world of zero trans-action costs, the efficient outcome always prevails. If people know what all their options are, understand exactly what attributes they are getting in a product, and know with certainty the outcome of each option, then it is an obvious conclusion that everyone will exercise their options in a way that makes them as well off as possible. No mutually beneficial transactions will be forfeited. In the software example discussed earlier, the bank would have known with certainty the probability of success of Rachel's software project and it would have lent the money to her. If the exchange process is not costless, however, then the efficient outcome will not occur. Mutually beneficial transactions will be left untapped.

Coase's work made the economics profession explicitly recognize the costless-exchange assumption that had been implicit in economic models. He demonstrated that the inefficient outcomes in neoclassical economic models derived not from assumptions about firm structure or other standard explanations but from the implicit presence of transaction costs. Let us examine two specific cases of inefficiencies, monopolies and externalities.

A *monopoly* exists when there is a single seller of a good or service. The U.S. Post Office has a monopoly on the delivery of parcel post, and local cable companies have monopolies in providing cable service to certain homes.[6] There is a common misconception that monopolists can charge any price they wish. We must remember, however, that the monopolist faces a downward sloping demand curve just like any other business. If a monopolist charges too high a price, it drives potential customers away. Moreover, regulators are more eager to intervene when they perceive that a business is abusing its monopoly position.

Economic theory holds that the profit-maximizing level of output for any firm is the point at which *marginal revenue* (MR), the addition to the total revenue of the firm from producing and selling the last unit, just equals the *marginal cost* (MC), the addition to total costs from producing the last unit. In Figure 3.1 this occurs at quantity Q*. The price the mo-nopolist charges is determined by the demand curve for the product, la-beled P* in the figure. The shaded triangle ABC is called the *deadweight loss* and represents the inefficiencies that monopolies generate. Why is this level of output inefficient? The monopolist charges price P* for the product—say $5. The marginal cost to the firm of producing one addi-tional unit is less than $5; in our example we assume that it is $3. So at output level Q*, there are potential consumers who would be willing to pay, say, $4 for the product. The firm would certainly be willing to sell

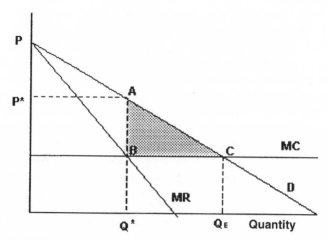

FIGURE 3.1   The Monopolist and Deadweight Loss

one additional unit at $4; since it would cost the firm only $3 to produce, profits would increase by $1. The firm would even be willing to produce one additional unit for a customer who was willing to pay $3.25; here the firm's additional profit would be $0.25. Efficiency in production occurs where price equals marginal cost. At this level of output, the firm's marginal profits from producing and selling the last unit is zero. In Figure 3.1 the efficient level of production is Q_E.

If the monopolist could isolate those customers who would purchase the product for more than $3 but less than $5, it could make side deals with them to purchase additional units at continuously reduced prices until the price equaled the marginal cost. Under this scenario, *the efficient outcome would prevail even in the monopoly setting.* In other words, the inefficiency does not result from the monopolist firm structure but from the difficulty the monopolist has in determining who those marginal customers are and in negotiating side deals with each of them. Because of the difficulty in making these exchanges, the standard monopoly result is the typical outcome. There are significant transaction costs for a firm to determine the preferences of individual consumers and then to contract with them individually. Moreover, these side deals must be kept secret, or all consumers will demand the lower price.

The second example of inefficiency involves an externality. A *negative externality* occurs when the social costs of production exceed the private costs of production to the firm, and the firm does not have to compensate those who bear the additional costs. An example of a negative externality is pollution. When a steel factory produces its output, a by-product is air pollution. Suppose the firm emits chemicals into the air that damage the exterior of homes near the factory. If the firm does not have to compensate the owners of the houses for the damage, then a negative externality exists. Figure 3.2 depicts the externality problem. The marginal benefits curve (MB) represents the additional benefits to society from production of the steel. The curve slopes downward because the additional benefits are very high when the firm produces the first units of steel, but the benefits fall (though they are still positive) as steel production increases. The benefits derive from the fact that the firm produces jobs and revenue and helps the community in a number of ways. The marginal private cost curve (MPC) represents the costs that the steel firm must pay—wages, rent, taxes, and so on. However, the firm does not have to pay for all of the costs that it imposes on society. In particular, the firm does not have to pay for the damage that its emissions cause to nearby homes. The firm produces at Q_A, where marginal benefits equal marginal private costs. This level of output maximizes profits for the firm.

From society's point of view, however, the efficient level of production is Q_E, where marginal benefits equal marginal *social* costs (MSC). The level Q_A is inefficient, because there are mutual gains from trade that are not being exploited. The homeowners could pay the polluting firm an amount greater than the additional profits the firm would receive on its last units of production but less than the amount of the damage done to the houses from the extra pollution, so that the firm would reduce steel production and pollution emissions from the factory. All parties would be better off, because the firm would make more profits and the damage to nearby houses would be reduced.

What prevents this solution from occurring is not the presence of the externality but the high transaction costs. The homeowners must coordinate with one another (negotiating costs), determine the amount of damage that the extra pollution is doing (measurement costs), and work out

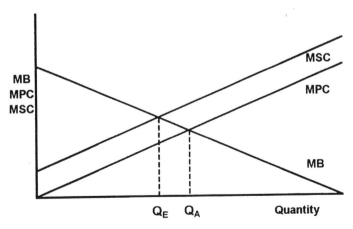

FIGURE 3.2   Negative Externality

a settlement with the firm (negotiating costs). The parties would then have to make sure that the agreement is honored (enforcement costs). This is a difficult and costly process. Only in a world of zero transaction costs does the efficient outcome prevail. Externalities only generate inefficiencies when there are positive transaction costs.

The inefficient outcomes associated with monopolies and externalities are only the tip of the iceberg. If an economy has high transaction costs, many potential exchanges are forfeited, and the economy operates well below the efficient level. Answers to many unexplained paradoxes become clearer. For example, why is it that investment in many developing countries remains so low despite all the potential gains? The neoclassical growth model suggests that marginal product of capital investment is high when the capital-to-labor ratio in a nation is low. Therefore, developing economies should have many latent investment opportunities with high returns. The answer is that many developing nations have high transaction costs that prevent these exchanges from occurring. Once we recognize the impact that transaction costs have on an economy, then we can better understand the solutions that are required to improve economic performance.

Link to Institutions

The Coase theorem can be related directly to the role of institutions in an economy, as illustrated in another example of transaction costs. A logging company and an environmental group are at odds over plans to log old-growth redwoods in the Pacific Northwest. The logging company owns the property rights to the forest, and those property rights allow the company to log the area. If there were zero transaction costs, the environmental group would determine how much it is worth to them to stop part or all of the logging. If that amount was greater than the marginal profits that the loggers could earn from their operations, the environmental group could purchase the property, and both parties are made better off. The efficient outcome prevails.

Suppose that transaction costs are present. The two groups are so bitterly opposed to one another that they cannot even talk to each other about the issues in a calm way. Moreover, the environmental group cannot agree on how much the forest is worth, and the loggers are unsure what their profits will be from logging. In this more realistic case, no transaction occurs and the loggers cut down the trees.

Now let us reverse the story. Loggers wish to cut trees on certain land, and the environmental group opposes the cutting. However, the environmental group owns the property rights to the land. In the absence of transaction costs, the loggers agree to purchase some or all of the land at a price higher than the environmental group's valuation of the trees, but at a low enough price that the logging is still profitable. Both parties are better off. Again, the efficient outcome prevails. But in the presence of significant transaction costs, such as those described above, the two parties cannot come to terms on any transaction, and the forest is not logged at all, because the environmental group refuses to grant any logging rights to the lumber company.

Two related points follow from this story. First, *if transaction costs are zero, the efficient outcome always prevails regardless of property rights assignments.* This is another way of stating the Coase theorem. No matter who initially owns the property rights to a good or service, trade will occur to make all parties better off. Second, *if transaction costs are positive, property rights assignments have a big impact on economic outcomes.* In the first transaction-cost scenario, the trees were logged; in the second, they were not. The assignment of property rights, first to the loggers, and then to the environmentalists, made the difference.

Recall that formal institutions are the written "rules of the game." In capitalism, property is privately held. Therefore, ownership rights to property must be clearly specified and enforced. One of the key roles of institutions is to define and enforce property rights. The corollary to the first proposition above is this: In a world of zero transaction costs, institutions do not matter. No matter what the institutional arrangements, people in the economy transact until all mutual gains from trade are exhausted. Aggregate production and income are always maximized even if income distribution is affected. But in the real world of positive transaction costs, institutions have a big impact on economic outcomes. The institutional framework of the nation determines how costly it is to transact and therefore determines the degree to which an economy attains its production and income potential. There is no question that transaction costs are always present and significant. Therefore, institutions always matter.

Questions for Discussion

1. What is meant by economic efficiency? What does efficiency have to do with the distribution of income in an economy?
2. Is the interest rate that you pay on your credit card a "transaction cost" as defined in this chapter? Why or why not?
3. What possible institutions could an economy create in order to lower transaction costs?
4. Suppose someone enters a room full of people and begins to smoke a cigarette, generating a negative externality with the second-hand smoke. Building codes specify that smoking is allowed in the room. What sort of agreement must be reached in order to eliminate the externality? What are the transaction costs that make it difficult to reach such an agreement?

Notes

1. The efficient outcome also prevails when all firms are perfectly discriminating monopolists, a subject discussed later.

2. Adam Smith, *An Inquiry into the Nature and Causes of the Wealth of Nations*, ed. Edwin Cannan (Chicago: University of Chicago Press, 1976), pp. 477–478.

3. Ronald H. Coase, "The Problem of Social Cost," *Journal of Law and Economics*, vol. 3 (October 1960), p. 15.

4. *New York Times*, "Modernization for Medicare Grinds to Halt," September 16, 1997.

5. Coase, "The Problem of Social Cost," pp. 1–44.

6. Determining whether or not a monopoly exists is not always an easy task. A monopoly exists only when reasonable alternatives to the good or service are not available. Cable companies would argue that in fact they do not have a monopoly because of competition from personal satellite dishes.

4

Institutions and Economic Growth: The Static Case

The Theory

We are now ready to integrate institutions, transaction costs, and economic performance as measured by per capita GDP. In this chapter we assume that technology is held constant. At any moment in time there is a given amount of technology that a nation has available to it. The nation need not improve its technology to grow; it simply needs to utilize the existing technology more efficiently. This scenario is represented in a production possibility frontier in Figure 4.1. Two goods are on the axes, good X and good Y. The curved line is the economy's frontier—that is, the maximum amount of production that an economy can produce using all of its available resources and the existing level of technology.[1] Production cannot occur beyond the frontier unless there is an increase in resources or an increase in the level of technology. Points on the frontier are efficient because the economy is utilizing its resources fully and making all the necessary exchanges in order to maximize production. If the economy is inside the production possibility frontier, however, the economy is inefficient. There are possible gains from trade that are going untapped. It could be that the economy has excess unemployment, so labor resources are sitting idle. If those resources could be employed, then economic growth would occur. Perhaps saving and investment are at low levels because there is a fear of nationalization of key industries. In either case, the economy can move from point A to point B in Figure 4.1 without any change in technology. Because technology is assumed to be unchanging over time in this model, we refer to this as the "static" case.

Figure 4.2 is a flow chart that illustrates how institutions affect economic performance, assuming the level of technology is held constant. Let us work through this flow chart backwards, from right to left.

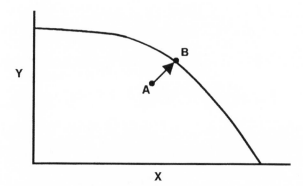

FIGURE 4.1   The Production Possibilities Frontier

Given the level of technology, a nation's standard of living is roughly determined by its GDP per capita. An increase in the standard of living requires an increase in average productivity by a nation's citizens. Productivity usually refers to output per unit of labor input, or output per hour of labor. Measured output is the market price of the good or service multiplied by the quantity produced. Labor input is measured by the number of hours worked. For example, if in five hours a worker produces ten calculators that sell for $30 each, output is $300 and labor input is five hours. Productivity is then $60 per hour. If the worker increases production to twelve calculators in five hours, output is $360 and productivity is $360 divided by 5 hours, or $72 per hour. The worker brings in more revenue for the firm, and under the right market conditions his or her wages and standard of living increase.

One way for workers to increase productivity is to increase the degree of specialization and division of labor. Suppose a firm produces automobiles. There are at least two ways to organize production. One is to assign a worker to a particular car in production and have that worker follow the car all the way through the production process. This worker assembles the engine, seats, steering wheel, windshield, doors, and so on as the car moves down the line. The worker inspects, cleans, and drives the car to the company parking lot.

The second method is to assign the worker to one particular task that he or she performs on every car that passes by. Obviously the second strategy is the more productive. Henry Ford built the first automobiles

Institutions ⇒ Transaction ⇒ Creation ⇒ Specialization ⇒ Productivity ⇒ Economic
                    Costs   of Markets   & Division   Performance
                                                  of Labor

FIGURE 4.2   The Static Case

with this method. Adam Smith observed the same concept in pin factories in the late eighteenth century. He wrote:

> [A workman] could scarce, perhaps, with his utmost industry, make one pin in a day, and certainly could not make twenty. But in the way in which this business is now carried on, not only the whole work is a peculiar trade, but it is divided into a number of branches, of which the greater part are likewise peculiar trades. One man draws out the wire, another straights it, a third cuts it, a fourth points it, a fifth grinds it at the top for receiving the head; to make the head requires two or three distinct operations; to put it on, is a peculiar business, to whiten the pins is another; it is even a trade by itself to put them into the paper; and the important business of making a pin is, in this manner, divided into about eighteen distinct operations. . . . [2]

This strategy of specialization allows a worker to learn one particular task very well. Over time the worker figures out the little secrets that make the job easier and develops the specific physical conditioning necessary to complete the task.[3]

The strategy of specialization carries some risk. As people become more and more familiar with their particular task, they lose (or never acquire) the ability to do many other tasks. An economics instructor knows how to teach economics, but she probably does not know how to grow her own food, build her house, sew her own clothes, or fix her car. If the markets were to collapse, most of us would have no idea even how to generate electricity. The point is that specialization and division of labor create a reliance on the market system to satisfy our various needs and desires. A construction worker knows how to build houses, but he buys clothes made in Nepal. His shoes are from Singapore, and his car from Japan.

In order to rely on the market, markets must exist and they must function well. We often take this for granted in the United States, but many markets in many parts of the world are simply nonexistent or work poorly. Why is it that in Kenya one cannot run to Wal-Mart at 3 A.M. to buy aspirin? The market does not exist. What is required for markets to exist and to function well? There are at least six criteria.

First, there must be consumer demand for the particular good or service. Demand is partially determined by the size of the market. In large cities, one finds an abundance of shops, malls, gas stations, lawyers, accountants, printers, and so on. Firms locate in large cities because consumers are there to purchase the goods and services. The approximate size of a firm in the long run is determined by economies of scale. If economies of scale are very large, each firm must produce large quantities of its product in order to achieve low average costs. If a market is small, firms cannot take full advantage of economies of scale and will not set up business in the area. This explains, for example, why big manu-facturing firms are not found in small towns. This does not mean that small towns have no markets. It simply means that the types of firms that locate there will be those with lesser economies of scale. Individual law practices take the place of big law firms in small towns.

Second, there must be suppliers. Usually for the market to function well, there must be numerous suppliers. Most suppliers enter the market only when they think they can make a profit. Total revenues must exceed total costs. Neoclassical economic theory teaches that costs are composed of capital and labor costs. Transaction costs are assumed to be zero. We now know that transaction costs are rarely zero and often are very sig-nificant. So total costs are the combination of labor, capital, and transac-tion costs (TC = labor costs + capital costs + transaction costs).

Ultimately, production is a combination of labor, raw materials, tech-nology, and a whole series of transactions. A producer takes raw materi-als and converts them into the end product. The producer must contract with owners of the raw materials, laborers, owners of the capital, whole-salers, retailers, and so on. Each of these transactions can be costly. Let us take the assembly of a typical computer as an example. The firm must contract with other producers to purchase the motherboard, the micro-processor, memory chips, disk drives, the monitor, the keyboard, the compact-disk player, the sound system, the computer's shell, and several software packages. The firm must then contract with workers to assem-ble the parts. Finally, the firm must have warehouse space, electricity, and telephone service and must contract with a trucking company to ship the finished products. If *any* of these links in the production chain is delayed, the production process either slows or stops completely.

The ability of the supplier to make a profit from assembling computers will depend in large part on the level of transaction costs. Are the mar-kets developed enough that the supplier can find reliable producers of all the component parts? Can the supplier negotiate prices that both parties agree on (negotiating costs)? Do the components meet the agreed-upon level of quality (measuring costs)? What happens if shipments are con-stantly late (enforcement costs)? What if a supplier refuses to pay? Is there a court system that will settle the dispute (enforcement costs)? Will the government nationalize the industry? The answers to these questions determine the level of transaction costs that the computer assembler faces. If the transaction costs are relatively low, it is likely that many com-puter assembly plants will be in operation. If transaction costs are high, few or no suppliers will enter the market.

The third criterion for well-functioning markets is that consumers must have good information about the price, quality, and attributes of the product. George Akerlof described this problem in the market for used cars.[4] When the consumer searches for a used car, transaction costs abound. The quality of the car is difficult to discern. Many of us have had the experience of purchasing a used car from an individual and finding that it needed hundreds of dollars of repair work just to pass the state inspection. Consequently, many people avoid the used-car market entirely. Would-be buyers do not purchase used cars from individuals for fear of being taken advantage of. And those who have high-quality cars to sell trade them in to dealers, because they do not want to go through the hassle of convincing potential buyers that their cars are really worth the price they are asking. The market for used cars would work well *if* the buyer could perfectly observe the condition of the car and determine how long the car will last and what sorts of repair expenses will be necessary in the future. But this information is only imperfectly known at best. One can take the car to an inspection center to obtain a mechanic's opinion. This costs money, and the mechanic may or may not be qualified. Hence the used-car market works poorly.

There are a few ways to partially overcome this measurement problem. First, the seller could offer a written warranty. Of course this warranty must be enforced by a court system. Second, the purchaser could ascertain the reputation of car dealers and deal only with those who get good reviews and have been in business for a long time. But the used-car market is inherently plagued with high costs of transacting.

Other markets have similar problems. The market for lawyers' services does not work as well as one might hope, because of the high costs of measuring a lawyer's performance and skills. A client has a difficult time of knowing whether he or she is getting good services for the price. The same is true for doctors. A patient rarely knows if the surgeon is truly qualified or inept at a given surgical procedure.

Fourth, there must be a stable monetary system that both the buyer and the seller recognize and trust. The U.S. dollar has been stable for more than a century. Dealing in dollars involves extremely low transaction costs. In fact, many citizens of other countries would rather deal in dollars than in their own countries' currencies, because their own currencies are not trustworthy. Often such currency weakness is a result of past or present hyperinflation (extremely high rates of inflation). Hyperinflation erodes the value of the currency and makes negotiating costs extremely difficult. Imagine that you loan someone $100, payable in one year. The year passes with an inflation rate of 100 percent. In real terms, the $100 you receive at the end of the year is worth half as much as the $100 initially loaned. In essence, you paid the borrower $50 to use your money. Commodity money, or paper money, arises out of a need to facilitate transactions. If the currency is stable and trustworthy, transaction costs are lowered.

Fifth, the seller must legitimately and securely hold the property rights to the good or service, and the seller must have the authority to transfer the property rights to the purchaser. One cannot legally sell something one does not own. If stolen property is resold, the transaction is not legal. Moreover, the seller must be able to transfer the legitimate property rights to the seller. If the consumer perceives a high risk of purchasing stolen property, transaction costs are increased. Also, if the property rights to the business or the assets are not secure, long-term planning and investment become very risky. Who would invest in an oil field if there is a high risk that the government will confiscate the land once oil is found? In many countries there are waves of *nationalization*, government takeovers of previously private assets. If a government has a history of nationalizing assets, investment within its jurisdiction becomes risky.

Finally, buyer and seller must have access to an impartial legal system in case one party cheats the other. Enforcement costs are perhaps the largest component of transaction costs. Many nations simply do not have adequate legal systems to enforce contracts, and so transactions are not secure. North identifies three types of markets. The first is personal exchange with no third-party enforcement. Exchange is primarily conducted between relatives and community members. With no system of outside enforcement, individuals must rely on the integrity of family relationships to honor agreements. The second is impersonal exchange with no third-party enforcement. This market has very high transaction costs, because there is no explicit bond between the parties to the exchange. Generally speaking, only parties who have long-term relationships or share religious and cultural values enter into contracts in such markets. The repeat dealings and shared norms help to keep each party honest. Neither of these two types of markets provides an adequate environment for exchange outside of community boundaries, because the transaction costs are too high. The third type of market is impersonal exchange with third-party enforcement. It is this market structure that is absolutely essential for the solid performance of modern capitalist economies.[5] Only in this setting will people routinely accept the risks inherent in exchange with people they do not know well. There must be a reliable arbiter of disputes to reduce the costs of exchange.

Markets function well if these six conditions are met, as a simple example will illustrate. Suppose Jane goes to a typical mall in the United States to buy a sweater. She walks in and out of several sweater shops and looks over the different designs and prices. She finally settles on one that she likes. Jane looks carefully at the tag to make sure it is 100 percent cotton. She feels the weight to gauge the sweater's durability. She looks for torn threads or any other defects. She is satisfied with the condition of the sweater and takes it to the counter. Someone is there to ring up and accept her payment. She pays by credit card, signs the charge slip, and goes home. One week later, after wearing the sweater once, Jane washes it and discovers that the colors have faded significantly. She drives to the mall, shows the sweater to the clerk, and demands a refund. Most likely, the salesperson refunds the money. If not, Jane can keep the sweater, drive home, write a letter to the bank that issued her credit card, and explain how she has tried in good faith to refund the sweater but the merchant has not cooperated. Again, the most likely outcome is that the bank takes the charge off her account and does not pay the merchant for the value of the sweater. If Jane had paid cash, she could have taken the merchant to small-claims court. In either case the property rights to that sweater were clear, and enforcement mechanisms existed to make this a routine transaction.

Suppose instead that Jane lives in Guatemala.[6] She drives to the market to purchase a sweater. There are a handful of different shops, but all carry very similar sweaters. Jane picks out her favorite one and checks for the tag but cannot find one. She then looks for any rips and feels the sweater's weight. The sweater seems to be fine. She purchases the sweater with cash and takes it home, and after washing it once the fabric rips. Jane returns to the market to exchange the sweater but the merchant refuses. Jane has nowhere to turn and takes the sweater home to mend it. Transaction costs are clearly higher in the second scenario. Jane will think twice before purchasing another sweater. The problem is magnified as the exchange becomes more complex.

Well-functioning markets require low transaction costs. With low transaction costs, exchanges are easier and more certain for both suppliers and consumers. How does an economy achieve low costs of transacting? A nation's institutional framework, the complex network of rules, customs, and enforcement systems, determines transaction costs. Governments play a fundamental role in determining how well an economy performs, since they are principally responsible for writing and enforcing formal rules. This idea turns *laissez-faire* (hands off) policy on its head. The typical ideology of those who advocate *laissez-faire* assumes that the government only gets in the way and obstructs the workings of a free market economy. When taken to the extreme, this leaves no room for government at all. But an economy with no government results in anarchy. Advocates of *laissez-faire* take for granted the government's role in defining and enforcing property rights. Economies *inherently* have high transaction costs because of the difficulty of human cooperation. Many people are honest and trust one another most of the time, but others are not honest and cannot be trusted to fulfill their end of agreements unless the proper incentives are in place. Therefore, the key economic role for the government may well be to create an institutional framework that lowers the costs of transacting. A well-functioning economy requires a well-functioning government.

Formal rules determine the level of transaction costs by their impact on measurement and enforcement costs. Measurement costs result from poor information about a product's attributes. Sellers will not typically disclose negative information about their products unless required to do so. They will also make exaggerated claims about their products. For this reason, formal institutions must force firms to represent their products accurately. For example, packaged food sold in the United States must include a list of all the ingredients and must indicate the nutritional content. Food can be labeled "low-fat" only if it meets certain criteria. When banks make loans they must follow truth-in-lending laws by accurately and uniformly quoting interest rates. Moreover, many regulations specify minimum quality or safety standards to which sellers must adhere. This allows the consumer to make certain assumptions about a product or service. For example, all physicians must go through an intensive training and examination process before they are licensed to practice medicine. This reduces the number of incompetent doctors, and so a patient's choice of a physician is not likely to be a choice between life and death. Similarly, home builders must meet all kinds of building, electrical, and plumbing codes so that the houses they build are reasonably safe from the hazards of fire and destruction from inclement weather.

Formal rules also help to create an enforcement mechanism. This is an extremely difficult task, but it is a crucial one to providing a framework for economic activity that has low costs of transacting. Enforcement requires an extensive legal system consisting of a police force, regulatory agencies, a court system, trained attorneys and judges, and prisons. The United States has one of the highest numbers of lawyers per capita in the world.[7] Many lawyers and judges spend their lives interpreting property rights and enforcing contract disputes. Imagine how the risks of exchange would increase if this entire legal system were nonexistent.

Though little has been said about them to this point, informal rules are an integral part of the institutional framework. In fact, they are probably much more important than formal rules, because culture is so pervasive that it greatly influences the type of formal rules we have and the way they are enforced. Informal institutions are the unwritten rules of society derived from culture and norms of behavior.

Lawrence E. Harrison has argued that culture is the dominant factor in determining whether or not an economy develops over time.[8] Whether a society will flourish or flop depends on the human creativity it fosters. A "better" culture is one that nourishes human creativity. To Harrison, four cultural factors are fundamental. First is the society's *radius of trust*. This is the degree to which a sense of natural community permeates the culture. With more trust, more respect is shown toward the individual, and consequently more of society's resources are devoted to human development. A broad radius of trust lowers transaction costs, because people generally believe that others will play by the rules and will not try to cheat each other. Harrison argued that the radius of trust in Latin America is very short. On a recent trip to Ecuador, I could sense this mistrust in a number of ways. First, buildings and houses in the large cities often look more like prisons from the outside. Most buildings have *rejas,* or grilled bars with sharp, pointed tops that serve as security barriers. Armed guards often reinforce the *rejas.* There is an ever-present fear that houses or businesses will be robbed. In fact, bank robberies in Ecuador occur at alarmingly high rates. Although the house I stayed in was in a relatively safe part of town, there were four locks to go through before one could enter the front door. The back of the house was protected by a tall concrete wall with sheared glass embedded on the top to discourage people from climbing over.

There is also a sharp distinction between family and nonfamily relationships in Latin America that differs from relationships in the United States. In Latin America, family is generally very tight, and most social activity revolves around family functions. This is in contrast to the breakdown of the family that we are seeing in the United States. However, Ecuadorians are deeply suspicious of those who are not family members. Guests are rarely invited into the home, and when they are, it is a big deal. This contrasts with the ease with which friends and acquaintances enter each other's homes in the United States.

Finally, I was speaking with a young businessman from the United States who had moved to Quito to work. He wondered what I was doing in Ecuador, and I explained that I was there to study transaction costs because I thought they were responsible for much of the disparities in living standards across nations. Before I could explain what I meant by transaction costs, he blurted out, "Tim, the real reason that living standards are low here is that nobody trusts each other." Without even trying, he had confirmed my belief that trust is an extremely important variable in how economies function.

The second cultural factor on Harrison's list is the rigor of the ethical system. This includes respect for the law and the inclination to follow the rules. It also determines the sense of social justice that a particular society has. Having a strong ethical system significantly reduces enforcement costs, because the people's ethical values constrain them from a host of harmful or illegal activities. There is a reduced chance of revolutions, guerrilla warfare, and the like if society feels that the economic system is treating people fairly. Moreover, no matter how large the government is, it cannot possibly detect and prosecute everyone who breaks the law. If many people simply ignore the formal rules, then order breaks down. In Russia, for example, most people do not pay their taxes. There is no way that the government can enforce tax laws when so many people ignore them. For order to exist, most people must want to obey the rules because of their own ethics.

The third cultural factor is the way in which authority is exercised. Is power viewed as something to be used and abused at the discretion of the leader, or is it something to be earned and used with wisdom to lead society to worthwhile goals? This has a profound impact on the creation and enforcement of efficient and equitable institutions. For markets to work well, enforcement by those in power must be relatively unbiased. It is easier to hire police officers and establish court systems than it is to get them to behave fairly and impartially. The concept of fairness varies across cultures. Is it fair for a police officer or a judge to take a bribe? I have lived my whole life in the United States and have never paid a bribe to anyone, but I spent a few months in Ecuador and had to pay a bribe to a police officer to pass my rental car through a toll booth even though the car was properly registered. Mexico recently fired 737 federal judicial police suspected of being involved in drug trafficking. In Colombia, where the police are ineffective at stopping terrorism and sabotage, oil companies have begun hiring the military to protect their assets.[9] Finally, in Nigeria, one of the world's largest oil producers, gas stations are routinely out of gas, and people wait days in line just to fuel their cars, because certain government officials profit from the domestic gasoline shortages.

This is not to say that the United States has a perfect enforcement system and that many other nations are teeming with corruption. I am suggesting, however, that the difference is a matter of degree. Relatively speaking, the U.S. justice system works well, and those of many transition and developing countries do not. It is difficult to legislate impartiality and fairness.

The final aspect of culture that Harrison identified is a society's attitudes regarding work, innovation, saving, and profit. Different cultures and religions have different attitudes toward these variables. Many ethnic groups have been referred to as "lazy" by members of Western cultures because of their different notion of time. The Western culture has an obsession with time and getting things done in an efficient manner. Many other cultures are less driven by task accomplishment and view time as something to pass enjoying the moment. It is pointless to argue which attitude is preferable, but the Western view undoubtedly leads to higher production and consumption levels. Some cultures focus on the past instead of the future. These cultures are less likely to promote saving and investment, because they see little opportunity or hope in the future. In the forward-looking society, saving and investment are ways to enrich oneself economically and simultaneously to advance standards of living. In the backward-looking society, profit is frowned upon as exploitation of the poor, perhaps because of past injustices that were imposed by the government or business owners. In the forward-looking society, profit is a just return for hard work and risk.

Informal institutions are slow to change. This does not mean that societies with the "wrong" culture are doomed to poverty.[10] A change in formal institutions can lead to a change in long-held cultural values and beliefs. For example, laws that give women equal employment opportunities may gradually alter the stereotypes that people have about women's role in society. Likewise, attitudes about corruption in government may change if sanctions against such corruption are made more severe. We must also be careful about blaming culture for a nation's poverty; here we run the risk of committing the fallacy of reverse causation, identifying "good" culture with wealthy economies and "bad" culture with poor economies. The real world is much more complex than that. There are traits in every culture that hinder growth, and there are traits that encourage growth. The real task of economic theory is to isolate those informal institutions that have a significant impact on economic performance. The four factors that Harrison suggested are a good place to begin.

Institutions affect transaction costs and economic performance. The flow chart in Figure 4.2 summarizes the story told in this chapter. Institutions must be created to reduce the costs of measuring and enforcing exchanges. Formal rules must clearly define the property rights to the goods or services being exchanged. Perhaps more important, the informal institutions of a nation must promote a sense of trust and respect for the rule of law. Finally, enforcement must be carried out as objectively and fairly as possible.

The institutional framework of a nation determines the level of transaction costs, which in turn determines how well markets function. The prevalence of well-functioning markets leads to a high degree of specialization and division of labor in the economy's markets. As with Adam Smith's pin factory, the more specialized and divided the tasks, the higher the level of productivity of workers. Higher productivity results in an increase in economic wealth.

Questions for Discussion

1. "Since transaction costs are the costs of making, measuring, and enforcing exchanges, institutions only affect consumers but not producers, because consumers are the ones who exchange their money for goods and services." Is this statement true or false? Explain.

2. Name five institutions that exist to lower the transaction costs of purchasing a house.

3. Do the concepts embedded in Christianity facilitate or inhibit the exchange process? Explain. Which major religion, Christianity, Judaism, or Islam, results in the lowest transaction costs? Why?

4. Do you think that relative to the rest of the world, the U.S. justice system is equitable? Why or why not? What impact does this have on economic performance in the United States?

Notes

1. Resources include land, labor, and capital. Land includes all the gifts of nature, such as oil, water, the fertility of soil, and so on. Labor includes all the human inputs into production, and capital includes all the human-made inputs into production, such as computers and machines.

2. Adam Smith, *An Inquiry into the Nature and Causes of the Wealth of Nations*, ed. Edwin Cannan (Chicago: University of Chicago Press, 1976), p. 8.

3. Of course there are mental and physical limits to one's ability to perform the same task over and over. The economic term for this is diminishing returns to scale.

4. G. A. Akerlof, "The Market for 'Lemons': Quality, Uncertainty, and the Market Mechanism," *Quarterly Journal of Economics*, vol. 84 (Spring 1970), pp. 488–500.

5. Douglass C. North, *Institutions, Institutional Change, and Economic Performance* (New York: Cambridge University Press, 1990), pp. 34–35.

6. This example is solely for illustrative purposes. All of the complications described may or may not occur in Guatemala, but they are more likely to occur in Guatemala than in the United States.

7. By some measures, the United States has the highest per capita number of lawyers. But other statistics show that the United States is third behind Japan and Germany. Nevertheless, these three countries have perhaps the highest living standards in the world. See Ian Van Tuyl, *Princeton Review Student Access Guide to the Best Law Schools* (New York: Random House, 1997). This should not imply that every lawyer service lowers transaction costs. Indeed, there is much rent seeking (lobbying the government for special treatment) that occurs that diverts society's resources into unproductive activities.

8. Lawrence E. Harrison, *Underdevelopment Is a State of Mind: The Latin American Case* (Lanham, MD: Center for International Affairs, Harvard University, and Madison Books, 1985).

9. *Christian Science Monitor*, "Massive Firing of Police in Mexico May Turn Some Into New Criminals," August 23, 1996, and *New York Times*, "Oil Companies Buy an Army to Tame Colombia's Rebels," August 22, 1996.

10. This does imply, however, that fundamental change may take a very long time. We return to this idea in Chapter 5.

5

Institutions and Economic Growth: The Dynamic Case

Institutions and Technological Change

In this chapter we relax the assumption that technology is fixed. We focus on a dynamic economy, one that is able to increase its level of technology over time. Assuming that an economy is operating efficiently, there are two ways to generate economic growth. One is to increase the amount of resources that go into the production process. This can occur as a result of the discovery of natural resources in the earth, an increase in population, an increase in machinery, and so on. In other words, if production inputs increase, so will output. This type of growth is called *extensive growth*. Since we are concerned with material standards of living measured by per capita output, extensive growth driven by population increases might not make us any wealthier on average.[1] Evidence suggests that extensive growth raises living standards very slowly.

Economic growth also comes from making our resources more productive. The higher productivity comes from advances in technology. This is called *intensive growth* because existing resources are used more intensively. Intensive growth is the key to raising living standards systematically over time. This concept is represented in the production possibility frontier in Figure 5.1. Holding the quantity of resources constant, an economy can move beyond the frontier only by increasing its technology. As technology improves, the entire frontier shifts outward toward the dotted line and society can produce and consume more goods and services than before.

How does an economy increase its technology over time? The development and integration of new technology are extremely complex. Here we address three key elements. First, a nation must foster human creativity. Individuals and firms must have the freedom and incentives to think about and experiment with new ideas. Society must be relatively

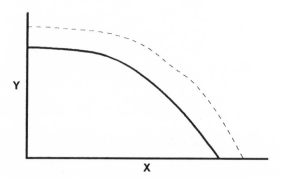

FIGURE 5.1   The Production Possibilities Frontier

open to change and willing to deal with the disruption in the status quo
that new technology brings. Different cultures and religions have varying levels of tolerance toward change. Many Middle Eastern countries resist Western-style change because of the disruption that it brings to society, and thus technological advancement is repressed.[2] Financial
incentives and rewards must accompany a high level of tolerance for creativity. Patents, for example, give monopoly rights to the developer for a
number of years. Pharmaceutical companies develop new drugs in part
because of the high returns they earn in the early years of the drug's production. Surprisingly, many studies show that although patents are important, they are not the most important factor in promoting creativity.

Government can also play a key role in the development of technology
by providing research and development funds to universities and re-
searchers. As technology becomes more complex, there is a high degree
of complementarity between technology and education. Nations that
have advanced educational systems do the best at developing and inte-
grating new technology into their economies, partly because educated
workers are more able to think for themselves and solve problems
creatively.

The second key element to advancing technology is a well-functioning
capital market. Converting an idea into a new or improved product is
often an expensive, risky process. The developer may not have access to
sufficient funds, and the needed start-up costs can be very high. The
process of channeling funds from savers to investors is inherently
plagued with high transaction costs, because savers cannot measure perfectly how their funds are being used; in addition, there is a risk of default. A country's institutions can lower these transaction costs by requir-
ing firms to accurately disclose financial information and by restricting
where and how funds are to be spent. The banking industry and the
stock market are two of the most highly regulated industries in the
United States because of the inherently high risks and poor consumer

information. Institutions such as deposit insurance requirements and information disclosure laws are necessary for a well-functioning capital market. When the capital market functions well, the economy's level of technology increases, because those with the ideas are better able to find financial support.

The third key element necessary for an economy to generate new technology is a competitive environment that forces firms to continually improve their products or risk being forced out of business. Joseph Schumpeter described the process eloquently in his famous book *Capitalism, Socialism, and Democracy*, first published in the early 1940s. He called it the process of *creative destruction*. Schumpeter wrote:

> The opening up of new markets, foreign or domestic, and the organizational development from the craft shop and factory to such concerns as U.S. Steel illustrate the same process of industrial mutation—if I may use that biological term—that incessantly revolutionizes the economic structure *from within*, incessantly destroying the old one, incessantly creating a new one. This process of Creative Destruction is the essential fact about capitalism. . . .
>
> But in capitalist reality as distinguished from its textbook picture, it is not [pure competition] which counts but the competition from the new commodity, the new technology, the new source of supply, the new type of organization (the largest-scale unit of control for instance)—competition which commands a decisive cost or quality advantage and which strikes not at the margins of the profits and the outputs of the existing firms but at their foundations and their very lives.[3]

Organizations under intense competition either improve their products with new technology, or they are squeezed out of the market. Today's computer markets are testimonies to this process. For decades IBM sat atop the computer world far ahead of competitors. But the firm recently lost $5 billion in a single year. Why? Competitors surged ahead in new products and technology and effectively destroyed the product line offered by IBM. Now IBM is the one playing catch-up.

Neoclassical economics preaches the virtues of perfect competition, an economy in which there is complete information about products, free entry and exit, and a large number of firms and consumers. In this environment, all firms earn normal returns. Firms are price takers because they have no price-setting abilities. The outcome is efficient, because price is equal to marginal costs. Schumpeter argued that the world of perfect competition is not necessary to achieve the process of creative destruction. In fact, perfect competition may hinder the process, because perfectly competitive firms have few resources left over in order to take risks and invest in new technologies. In theory, if one firm takes a risk and fails, it will be driven out of business immediately. Oligopolies (industries with a few big sellers) may be more apt to engage in the process of creative destruction.

The process of creative destruction is analogous to Darwin's theory of evolution. Darwin argued that stronger species are better able to adapt to their environments and drive out inferior species through the process of natural selection. If a species cannot respond to a key change in its environment, it will become extinct. Likewise, an organization that does not continually respond to changes in its environment will be driven out of business by a competitor.

The flow chart in Figure 5.2 shows how institutions affect economic performance through time. Institutions influence the behavior of organizations, which leads to the process of creative destruction. This process advances technology and leads to an increase in economic wealth.

The process of creative destruction does not occur in every economy. It only occurs when the proper institutional framework is present. Recall that institutions provide the framework under which organizations operate. Economic organizations seek to maximize profits, but they could do so in a number of ways. Firms could lobby their government for protection via tariffs, quotas, and regulations; they could secure a monopoly position by buying up or forcing out competitors; they could gain cost advantages by ignoring environmental laws or labor laws; or they could be forced to maximize profits by increasing technology and producing an ever-more competitive product. This last alternative is the one that leads to the process of creative destruction.

The key is for the institutional framework to constrain firms' activities enough so that the main way for them to make a profit is by increasing technology. A good analogy is to think of the institutional framework as the walls of a maze. The maze must be set up to close off all possible paths but a few. If a firm goes down the wrong path, it must turn back and try another one. The main path that must be open in an economy is the one that encourages competition and discourages special treatment and government protection. A successful economy must be *adaptively efficient*.[4] It must be able to overcome shortages of resources or other bottlenecks by being able and willing to find new and creative solutions. If one path does not work, there must be organizational responses that try new paths until successful outcomes are achieved.

Technology progresses from both microinventions and macroinventions. *Microinventions* are "the small, incremental steps that improve,

Institutions $\Rightarrow$ Behavior of $\Rightarrow$ Process of $\Rightarrow$ Technological $\Rightarrow$ Economic
                          Organizations   Creative   Progress   Wealth
                                               Destruction

FIGURE 5.2   The Dynamic Case

adapt, and streamline existing techniques already in use, reducing costs, improving form and function, increasing durability, and reducing energy and raw material requirements. *Macroinventions,* on the other hand, are those inventions in which a radical new idea, without clear precedent, emerges. . . . "[5] Microinventions and macroinventions are complementary, not interchangeable. Rapid technological progress occurs when individuals throughout the economy have incentives to apply the knowledge that they have accumulated to improve the production process. There must also be those select visionaries who discover and create entirely new ideas. A country's institutions are vital to these processes. Patents are necessary for the firm to earn rents from the invention, but the organization itself also must reward its creative employees. Organizations that thrive in the long term are those that allow workers to contribute to solutions by offering pecuniary or nonpecuniary incentives. Economic historians have found that the rapid rise in living standards during and especially after the Industrial Revolution was primarily the result of countless gradual inventions by many unknown people; it was not the result of a few major inventions, as we sometimes think. Perhaps the single greatest pitfall of socialist economies was the lack of incentives for people in organizations to contribute to the technological progress, an idea that is discussed in detail later.

Institutions themselves cannot be stagnant. They must constantly evolve and respond to different circumstances. For example, a major issue brought to the fore by the explosive growth of the Internet is intellectual property rights. Now it is possible for someone in China to copy a piece of work from someone in Canada in a matter of seconds. Software, CDs, and videos can easily be copied and sold illegally. How should intellectual property be protected? If the requirements are too stringent, then access to information and markets is limited. If the requirements are too loose, then incentives to create intellectual works are reduced. The accessibility of information via the Internet means that institutions must change in order to keep pace.

Institutions change in part because organizations influence them. Many formal institutions are created by the legislative branches of governments. Organizations lobby and otherwise influence this process. If organizations gain too much influence, they can inhibit competition in their industries and slow the march of technology. Institutions must foster creativity, lower transaction costs in capital markets, and encourage the process of creative destruction.

The Persistence of Poor Economic Performance

Why do so many nations *remain* persistently poor? We saw in Chapter 1 that the gap between many rich and poor nations is actually widening, despite the massive flows of technology made possible by today's information and communication resources. Why don't nations imitate other nations' successes by modeling their institutional structure after the wealthier economies? Even if a country's institutions are not conducive to growth initially, it seems like a country could change its institutional framework over time in a way that promotes growth.

There are at least three reasons for the persistence of poverty decade after decade, often century after century. First, economies are *path dependent*. This term implies that once an economy is on a particular path, it is very difficult to change paths. Organizations adapt to the existing structure and resist changes. Many people, including politicians who create most of the formal institutions, benefit from the status quo. A radical reorganization of institutions radically alters income distribution. Those with wealth and power will not let this happen without a fight. Hence, organizations become comfortable with the ways things are, and they become a built-in source of resistance to change.

An analogy with technology illustrates the concept of path dependence. Microsoft's DOS operating system was clearly inferior to the Macintosh system with its graphical user interface. For nearly ten years, Microsoft lagged behind in developing user-friendly software, yet its sales surged ahead of Apple's. This is because many businesses adopted the DOS software first, purchasing machines made by IBM and other producers. Once the initial investment of computers and software was made and employees became comfortable working with the DOS system, it was too difficult and expensive to change, even though the Macintosh system was better. Ironically, it is Apple that is struggling to stay in business. The company failed to attract enough major purchasers of its systems to gain a solid market share.

The story of VHS and Beta videotapes is similar. Beta tapes are more durable and more compact. Yet VHS tapes have driven Beta tapes out of the market because so many VCRs were built to handle the VHS system. Once consumers purchased the VCRs, it was too expensive to switch to the Beta system. The layout of typewriter keys and computer keyboards offer another example. Engineers have studied keyboard layouts and have redesigned them to increase typing efficiency. Secretaries who use the new systems are able to type much more efficiently than those using the QWERTY keyboard. Why then aren't all keyboards changed? Because people have used the older system for so long that the costs of changing over are too high. Economies go through similar experiences. Once a new technology or institutional arrangement is put into place, the economy adapts to it. It becomes very difficult to change despite the potential gains.

The second reason for the persistence of poverty is that we do not know exactly what advice to give particular countries. This is because we have yet to understand the complex interactions between institutions and economic performance. Moreover, human beings do not possess the mental capabilities to understand completely how our world works. The information we use to make decisions is limited at best, but typically it is nonexistent or even wrong. The lack of information and the complexity of the world make it difficult for us to assess the impacts that different institutions will have on economic performance. In other words, the people living and working in economies that function well cannot explain very well what they are doing right, and those in economies that function poorly cannot explain what they are doing wrong. Scholars who spend lifelong careers analyzing economies often cannot agree on something as simple as the impact of tax rate changes on labor supply. With so much uncertainty, how can a country know what to do?

These uncertainties make it possible for wildly differing ideologies to appear and persist alongside one another. Marxian and dependency theories are two ideologies that persist alongside neoclassical economics. If we had perfect information and the mental capabilities to understand the world perfectly, incorrect ideologies would quickly be cast aside. We would be able to see cause-and-effect relationships and root out the institutions and ideologies that keep economies poor. But in our complex world, ideas matter. Policies are often written and implemented on the basis of the way we view the world, and on the basis of what we *think* will happen. The actual results may be very different.

The third factor in explaining the persistence of poor economic performance is that informal institutions evolve very slowly over time. Suppose that one culture possesses characteristics that foster economic growth, and another culture does not. As the cultural traits are passed from generation to generation, economic performance tends to repeat itself. It may take years, decades, or even centuries for informal institutions to evolve into traditions that promote economic growth. It may be necessary to expose a nation to foreign cultures and influences in order to speed up the process of cultural change. Spain is a prime example of this. From the eighteenth century through the 1960s, Spain was economically and culturally behind its European counterparts. It is hard to imagine today, but Spain was ruled by a dictator (Generalissimo Francisco Franco) until 1975. Spain began in the 1950s to open itself up to Western Europe and the United States through trade, investment, and tourism.[6] Though Spain is still one of the poorer countries in Western Europe, it has radically transformed itself. In a testimony to how far Spain has come, it is one of the initial eleven nations to be included in the monetary unification of Europe under a single currency, the *euro*.

In order for an economy to achieve intensive growth over time, its technology must increase. This requires an institutional framework that promotes individual creativity, well-functioning capital markets, and the process of creative destruction. However, there is nothing to guarantee that a society's institutions will adapt over time in an efficient manner. Path dependence, the gap between the world's complexity and our ability to understand it, and the slow evolution of informal institutions allow economies to march down inefficient paths indefinitely. In other words, there is no guarantee that institutions will ever evolve to tap the latent wealth of a nation. This is a sobering thought but one that fits the facts of our world quite well. Many nations of Central America, Africa, and Southern Asia seem to be stuck in a mode of economic stagnation. Economies can be permanently stuck in a low-growth mode with lagging technology.

Questions for Discussion

1. Can technology solve the world's problems? Explain.
2. Think of one other example of how an inferior technology has won out over a superior technology. Explain why this has happened.
3. Of the three reasons listed in the chapter to explain the persistence of poor economic performance, which one is the most important? Explain.
4. Is there hope for many of the world's economies? Why or why not?

Notes

1. In fact, there is a correlation between poverty and high population growth. Women in wealthier nations have fewer children than women in developing countries. Although the high population growth in poor countries means that economic growth is probably occurring as a result of the increase in the resource base, per capita growth may be stagnating or even declining.

2. This repression may be "good" for a nation if it is trying to preserve or enhance certain values. However, the slowdown in technology will also lead to slower rates of increase in standards of living.

3. Joseph A. Schumpeter, *Capitalism, Socialism, and Democracy* (New York: Harper & Row, 1950), pp. 83–84.

4. Douglass C. North, *Institutions, Institutional Change, and Economic Performance* (Cambridge: Cambridge University Press, 1990), p. 80.

5. Joel Mokyr, *The Lever of Riches* (New York: Oxford University Press, 1990), p. 13.

6. Lawrence E. Harrison, *Underdevelopment Is a State of Mind: The Latin American Case* (Lanham, MD: Center for International Affairs, Harvard University, and Madison Books, 1985), p. 139.

6

The Polity as Creator of Institutions

Chapters 4 and 5 elaborated on the key role that institutions play in determining economic performance. Up to now, we have not considered the origins of these institutions. Formal institutions and enforcement mechanisms are not created in a vacuum. Most of these institutions come from the political sector, the state. Focusing on institutions without examining their ultimate source leaves the theory of the New Institutional Economics incomplete.

Some economies seem to produce relatively efficient institutions, whereas many others do not. It seems a logical deduction, then, to suppose that some political systems are able to produce more efficient institutions than others. This chapter models the political system and answers three related questions. First, why do so many polities produce inefficient institutions? Second, what types of political systems are the most likely to produce efficient economic institutions? Third, how can a nation limit corruption in government? The answers to these questions have profound implications. If the root source of economic inefficiency lies in the way that political systems are organized, then a restructuring of political institutions and organizations is a necessary condition for reversing poor economic performance. Political and economic reforms have to be implemented in tandem. Economic reform may be impossible without political reform because the existing political structure cannot produce the necessary economic institutions.

More than 200 years ago James Madison, Alexander Hamilton, and John Jay wrote a series of articles designed to persuade New York voters to ratify the U.S. Constitution. Collectively these essays—reprinted many times since then—became known as the Federalist Papers. In the tenth essay of the series, referred to as Federalist No. 10, James Madison eloquently described the destabilizing effect that factions can have on society, and he argued that the U.S. Constitution would limit the destabilizing power of factions by the establishment of a republic. The main question that he addressed is the following: How can the interests of particular factions be kept in check such that the will of the faction does not override the common good? The faction could be a minority or a majority of the population. Factions arise from the differences in individual values, beliefs, and goals. Business owners, for example, have different interests than wage earners. Liberals have a different view of the world than conservatives. A successful political system must mute the power of factions so that their will cannot dominate the broader public interest. The system would limit, for example, the ability of the ruling party to reap profits by granting monopoly rights to particular firms. Or it would limit the ability of the wealthy to shift their tax obligations to other citizens.

Governing bodies themselves can become factions that destabilize an economy. Governments are necessary to define and enforce the rules of the game in society. The problem is that a "government strong enough to protect property rights and enforce contracts is also strong enough to confiscate the wealth of its citizens."[1] In other words, there is a tension among governing bodies either to nurture economies to grow by facilitating exchange or to confiscate assets and wealth outright. In a general sense the first scenario is referred to as the contract theory, and the second, as the predatory theory.[2] States in history have played both roles. But there are differences between the two models. The contract theory requires time to allow economies to grow and a viable tax system that allows the state to reap the fruits of its patience. The predatory theory provides the rulers with short-term gains but wipes out dynamic incentives for citizens to accumulate wealth via the production of goods and services.

The predatory theory prevails more often when the ruler has a short-term outlook or an urgent need for short-term revenue (e.g., financing a war). The predatory model is also the more likely outcome when the tax system functions so poorly that the best way for revenue to be transferred to the state is for assets to be confiscated directly. In contrast, the contract theory is feasible for a governing body with a long-term horizon, adequate sources of revenue, and a well-functioning tax system that transfers income from the private to the public sector.

Beyond these characteristics, there is a time inconsistency problem. A state could claim that it is following the contract theory, but when its citizens have built up sufficient levels of wealth, the state could then confiscate the assets. If a nation's citizens are rational, they will foresee the possibility that the state could confiscate their wealth at any point in the future. This should dampen incentives for economic growth. The key issue is that the state cannot credibly commit to not confiscating wealth in the future no matter how long its time horizon or how good its access to revenue.

Clearly the contract theory provides the basis for long-term economic growth. If a nation is to achieve high standards of living, the political system must create institutions that facilitate market development, and it must encourage the formation of organizations that engage in Schumpeter's process of creative destruction. But short-term demand for wealth leads the state to confiscate assets and undermine economic performance. We must explore the types of political systems that can credibly commit the state to follow the contract theory. If there is no viable predatory option for a state, then the government must facilitate exchanges and promote market development if it wishes to increase its wealth. There are an infinite number of possible political systems. We explore only three of these: a state that consists of a single sovereign ruler, a political system ruled by a single congressional body, and a federalist system. We turn now to an examination of the types of institutions that these three political systems are likely to produce.

The Sovereign Ruler

Imagine a nation ruled by one leader, who has sole discretion over creating most formal institutions in the economy. We assume that the goal of the sovereign is to maximize his or her personal wealth.[3] The ruler will act like a discriminating monopolist by separating the nation's constituents into distinct groups and creating formal institutions that extract the maximum amount of revenues from each group.[4] Constituents who have little political power and little ability to hide their output from the ruler (small farmers, for example) will be heavily taxed. Those who have more political influence and those whose income can more easily avoid detection by the ruler will be given more favorable treatment.

The ruler always has competition for power. Competition can come from powerful persons in the nation or from other nation-states. If there is a low degree of competition, then there are few constraints on the ruler's behavior, and he or she can more heavily extract resources from citizens. If there is a high degree of rivalry for power, then the range of activities that the ruler can carry out is more constrained. In particular, the ruler will have to appease the powerful interest groups with favorable treatment. In either case, the result is a set of inefficient institutions that benefit the ruler and the powerful interest groups in the society at the expense of the marginalized. Moreover, if the transaction costs of measuring output and enforcing tax laws are high, then the ruler will likely trade monopoly rights for revenue. Interest groups that the ruler must please will tend to obtain these rights. This leads to more inefficient institutions and unproductive organizations. In short, a political system that consists solely of a sovereign ruler is prone to behave as a predator and is strongly biased to produce inefficient institutions that lead to a poorly performing economy.

This suggests that there should be a negative relationship between strong rulers and economic growth. Indeed, a casual look at economic history seems to confirm this. Spain was the dominant world power in the sixteenth century, but its obsession with royal centralization led to an inefficient bureaucracy and a stagnant economy while the Netherlands and then Great Britain surged ahead. Many Latin American nations in the past two centuries have had dictatorships that put private wealth ahead of economic gain. The corruption of the Somoza regime in Nicaragua and the stagnation of Argentina under Perón are perhaps the most famous cases. These two countries experienced dismal economic performance under their respective dictators. In the 1997 Index of Economic Freedom compiled by the Heritage Foundation, countries were rated along a continuum from "free" to "repressed." The authors then plotted the growth rate of real per capita GDP between 1976 and 1991 against the freedom index.[5] The results show a strong negative correlation between growth and repression.

However, the negative relationship between strong rulers and economic growth is not always definitive. There are many exceptions to the rule. India has had relatively poor economic performance despite establishing a stable democracy in 1947. The strong economic performances of Chile, Korea, Singapore, Taiwan, and China have all come under various degrees of ruler sovereignty. Indeed, many argue that the success of these economies would have been impossible *with* democracy. The radical changes that took place in society as a result of shifting jobs, incomes, and traditions would have been too much too fast, and a democratic government would have slowed down or halted the change. Lee Kuan Yew, Singapore's leader, said in 1992, "I do not believe that democracy necessarily leads to development. I believe that what a country needs to develop is discipline more than democracy. The exuberance of democracy leads to indiscipline and disorderly conduct, which are inimical to development."[6]

Despite the exceptions, there is a long-term correlation between democracy and economic growth. A more careful analysis of economic reform suggests that democratic governments are often just as able or more able than authoritarian regimes to carry out radical reforms. Australia (1983), Colombia (1989), New Zealand (1984), Poland (1990), Portugal (1985), and Spain (1982) provide examples of successful reform by democratic governments.[7] The point is that dictators (like elected governors) still have to worry about pleasing certain constituencies and therefore cannot make any change at will. A strong democratic system may be able to support more change than a weak dictator can support.

Empirical studies have shown that economic and political freedom promote economic growth. Why is this so? A benevolent dictator may get the institutions and economic policy right, which leads a nation down a high-growth path. But those institutions and policies are not secure through time. The dictator could suddenly change course or be replaced by another ruler who is not so friendly toward markets. Democracies are certainly not insulated from being overthrown, but the likelihood is small. Democratic systems are set up such that change must be approved by a number of people. This makes it more difficult to radically change course when policies are benefiting the constituents. Therefore, over the long term, efficient economic institutions are more stable in democracies than in other systems.[8]

It is more difficult in democracies than in dictatorships for particular factions to impose their will on society. A sovereign ruler or even a series of rulers may operate under the contract theory, but eventually a ruler will succumb to the temptation for short-term wealth and begin acting as a predator. Therefore, a sovereign ruler tends to produce economically inefficient institutions, which hinders economic performance.

The Congress

A second possible political system is a single elected congressional body. In history, sovereign rulers have often found themselves in a revenue bind. The ruler may have needed revenue to finance a war or to fund a large public project. In exchange for revenue from the nobility or the land-owning class, the ruler agreed to sacrifice some political power. Over time political power initially embedded in the aristocracy and nobility evolved into a formal body of government that we generically call a "congress." In this political system, each representative has constituents that he or she must please in order to obtain sufficient votes to remain in office. The congress listens to the constituents and then creates and passes legislation.

Will institutions that promote good economic performance be created in such a system? A useful benchmark is the "efficient" political system, a system that operates in such a way that leads to efficient economic outcomes. According to North,

> An efficient political market would be one in which constituents could accurately evaluate the policies pursued by competing candidates in terms of the net effect upon their well-being; only legislation (or regulation) that maximized the aggregate income of the affected parties to the exchange would be enacted; and compensation to those adversely affected would insure that no party was injured by the action.[9]

In this hypothetical environment, society would maximize its aggregate income because all legislation that increased aggregate income would be passed, and anyone who was harmed from such legislation would be compensated. No one would be made worse off, yet all mutual gains from political exchange would be exhausted.

Like economies, all polities fall far short of this efficiency ideal. There are many stumbling blocks along the way to creating efficient legislation, mainly because of the presence of transaction costs. Let us begin with the notion that legislation is supposed to reflect the preferences and values of the constituents. Because there is a great deal of uncertainty in trying to discern what constituents desire, legislators often must make an educated guess on the basis of limited information. Moreover, there are always differences of opinion among constituents. When a legislator is faced with a binary yes/no vote, any decision will alienate a portion of the constituents. There is also the principal/agent issue. A legislator who acts on an agenda that reflects his or her own values and beliefs, independently of those of the constituents, is acting as a principal rather than an agent. A legislator may vote to defeat an abortion bill, for example, because she believes that abortion is wrong regardless of what her constituents believe. Thus what the constituents really want and what the legislator tries to deliver will not necessarily be identical.

The representatives must then negotiate with each other in order to produce the legislation. Such a process is plagued with high transaction costs. Legislators must make exchanges that are extremely complex and diverse and that span time. One representative may promise to support another's tax bill in exchange for support on a future welfare bill. How does one go about measuring the attributes involved and then enforce such an exchange? Political exchange by necessity requires comparing apples and oranges. Reputation and repeat dealings help in the self-enforcement of exchanges, but they are not sufficient, because it is difficult at times to discover who is cheating whom and then to determine who should be the one to punish those who cheat. In order to better structure exchange, congressional bodies have developed elaborate committee structures in which certain legislators have control over specific areas of the economy.[10] In this way, exchange among politicians becomes easier because legislators can more readily identify whom they will be negotiating with over various issues. Exchanges do not begin in a vacuum each time. Committee structures reduce but by no means eliminate the transaction costs of political exchange.

Even if legislators acted in the true interests of their constituents, and even if legislators could make the exchanges necessary to pass the desired legislation, there is another fundamental problem. The world is extremely complex, and information is incomplete; therefore, constituents and legislators must construct subjective mental models in order to explain the world around them. This leads to ideological differences and outcomes that are sometimes very different from those intended. Recall that an efficient political system would enact all legislation that would maximize aggregate income. In reality, we often do not know whether a proposed bill will maximize aggregate income or not. We have to rely on our best estimate. Moreover, the legislation will affect so may people in varying degrees that we cannot even begin to assess the costs and benefits completely.

Finally, political efficiency requires that we compensate the losers in a political exchange—those who are harmed by it. Again, transaction costs prevent us from accurately identifying those who are harmed. Even if we could determine who is worse off from the exchange, it is usually impossible to determine how much they were harmed. This is especially true when legislative bills lump together all sorts of different exchanges. One component of the bill may make my situation better, but another may harm me. Disentangling all these impacts is usually impossible.

Despite these complications, an elected congressional body will likely produce institutions that are more efficient than those produced under a sovereign ruler because the congressional representatives must please their constituents. The process of negotiating and exchanging political favors will impose some restraints on the congressional system because the different legislators will fight for their own projects. It is more difficult for one legislator or a small group of legislators to impose their own will on the majority. Yet a congressional body will still produce institutions that are far from efficient, because of the transaction costs involved in going from constituents' preferences to actual legislation.

There is another problem with a political system composed of one congressional body. How is the congress's power reined in? Let us return to the contract and predatory theories of the state. How is the congress prevented from acting like a predator and confiscating wealth from its citizens? Assuming the congress is wealth-maximizing, there will be a tendency for it to extract revenue from citizens (especially citizens from other districts) in order to fund projects in the congress's interest. Such predatory behavior discourages incentives for markets to develop and reduces economic growth.

The fact that there is a large number of legislators makes it difficult for the congress to agree on the type of predatory behavior it wishes to pursue, but predatory behavior itself is not a problem. What keeps current members of congress from changing the democratic rules of the game and passing legislation, for example, that extends the length of term in office or gives incumbents even more of an advantage through campaign finance laws? This problem goes to the heart of maintaining the balance of power between a government and its citizens, and we will return to it in detail in the next section. Despite the improvements of a congress over a sovereign ruler, a congressional body is still likely to produce inefficient institutions, because of the transaction costs involved in translating constituents' demands into legislation. Moreover, there is no clear limit to congress's predatory power. We turn now to a third possible form of political organization called market-preserving federalism.

Market-Preserving Federalism

Federalism is a political system defined by two characteristics.

1. There is a hierarchy of government, with at least two distinct levels, each with its own defined scope of authority.

2. Institutions exist to render the autonomy of each level of government self-enforcing. In other words, a sustainable federalist system must prevent the higher level of government from overcoming or absorbing lower levels.[11]

For example, the United States has three broad levels of government: national, state, and local. The U.S. Constitution and federal and state laws define the scope of authority that each level possesses.

These two conditions necessitate a distinction of governmental powers, but they say nothing about the scope of authority over economic issues. Barry R. Weingast has specified three additional conditions necessary for *market-preserving federalism:*

3. Subnational governments have primary responsibility over the economy in their jurisdictions.

4. A common market is ensured, preventing lower-level governments from creating artificial trade barriers within the nation.

5. Lower-level governments face hard budget constraints, which means that they have to live within their means; they do not have the ability to print money or have access to unlimited credit.[12]

These five conditions assure that the government preserves markets. Why is this so? Let us focus first on the third and the fifth market-preserving conditions. Lower levels of government make economic policy, but as long as there is a reasonable degree of capital and labor mobility, subnational governments are constrained in their ability to place excessive burdens on their local economies. This is because one subnational government competes with other subnational governments for economic resources. In the case of the United States, for example, if the state of California or the county of Marin places too many regulations or burdens on its economic organizations, these organizations would be free to move to other political jurisdictions.[13] Therefore, economic institutions must be formed with the knowledge that other political systems are able and willing to absorb economic organizations if the institutions are too severe. This does not mean that all jurisdictions will look the same, nor that laissez-faire will reign everywhere. Since individuals and organizations differ in tastes and preferences, the types of economic regulation that evolve will also differ. But the important point is that people and organizations are free to vote with their feet, and this mobility limits the regulations that subnational governments can place on economic activity. In order to make sure that subnational governments feel the effects of their institutions, a hard budget constraint is necessary. If the federal government bailed out Orange County, for example, every time it ran into fiscal trouble, then local legislators could act with less concern for the consequences of their policies. It is competition combined with fiscal discipline that limits political authority over markets.

The fourth market-preserving condition, the common-market constraint, is necessary to ensure that subnational governments do not build their own economic nation-states. Political groups in the subnational governments will have incentives to erect trade barriers and otherwise protect their own organizations from the harmful effects of competition. But to ensure economic efficiency, the higher level of government must prevent this. The "commerce clause" in the U.S. Constitution gives the federal government vast power to regulate commerce "with Foreign nations, and among the several states. . . . " This clause prohibits states from erecting trade barriers between one another or between a state and another nation, guaranteeing a single, integrated economy.

To this point, we have not sufficiently addressed the tension between the contract theory and the predatory theory embedded in condition 2 above. Even if market-preserving federalism is established, what prevents the national government from overwhelming the subnational governments? For example, even if the federal government of the United States initially grants economic authority to the states, what prevents it from overstepping its bounds in the future, reducing state power, and assuming more control over economic events? Simply dividing the government into hierarchical units is not sufficient, because the hierarchy need not be honored. Indeed, in many developing countries, newly elected governments frequently rewrite the nation's constitution to redefine the levels of government to their own liking. What we are searching for is a self-enforcing equilibrium in which it is in the national government's interest to honor the institutions of market-preserving federalism. That is, if the government tries to overstep its bounds, there will be serious repercussions.

Weingast argues that there are two conditions necessary to achieve such a self-enforcing equilibrium. First, the citizens of a nation must hold sufficiently similar views about the appropriate bounds of government. There must be a strong consensus about what the proper role of the government is and should be. Second, if the government oversteps those bounds, the citizens of that nation must be able and willing to punish the government.[14] Only if these conditions are met will the government voluntarily stay within its appropriate bounds.

These two conditions are very difficult to achieve. Nations that have a great deal of heterogeneity and ethnic diversity will have a hard time forming a consensus about the proper role of government. In such an environment, the theory suggests that governments can get away with severe abuses. Military dictatorships ruled Argentina and Chile in the

1970s. Such a scenario is unthinkable in the United States, Canada, or Great Britain, for example. One cannot help but wonder at the reaction citizens in the United States would have if the president were to announce the formation of a dictatorship, or if he were to abolish the Congress, as President Boris Yeltsin did recently in Russia. It is clear, however, that there would be a swift, angry, and possibly violent reaction from citizens. This would not be acceptable government behavior, and the president would lose credibility. In the final analysis, a nation's citizens must define the appropriate limits of governmental authority, and they must be prepared to act when those boundaries have been crossed. Such self-enforcing limits combined with market-preserving federalism ensure that the contract theory, and not the predatory theory, becomes the main mode of operation in the political system. Note that this self-enforcing limit to governmental authority can result whether the leadership is a single ruler, a single congressional body, or a federalist system. But a ruler and a single congressional body still will not likely produce institutions that are market preserving. Given the absence of competition for economic resources, rulers and the congress would still create institutions that cater to certain interest groups with no particular concern for market efficiency.

The five conditions of market-preserving federalism, which require a general consensus by the nation's citizens over appropriate government boundaries and a willingness to enforce those boundaries, result in a political system that respects markets. In this environment markets can develop without fear of excessive wealth confiscation by the political sector. As such, market-preserving federalism encourages the creation of formal institutions that lead to economic growth.

Limiting Corruption

All governments are susceptible to corruption. Yet some governments, such as those in the United States and United Kingdom have a reputation for being relatively free of corruption. Other governments are famous for their excesses. Brazil's President Fernando Collor, for example, resigned in 1992 after accusations of illegally profiting from business dealings. The recent history of Uganda under Idi Amin is a story of how one ruler single-handedly destroyed the credibility of that nation's government. Corruption in Russia is endemic, and business dealings in China are extremely difficult if one does not pay bribes.

The primary economic role of the state is to create an institutional environment that facilitates exchange and creates dynamic incentives for growth. Corruption directly undermines that role by diminishing the credibility of the state and by weakening the legitimacy of the formal rules imposed by the government. After all, if government officials do not play by the rules, why should anyone else? Corruption also magnifies the perception that the rules of the game are not fair; hence many citizens become bitter and distrustful toward the government and its agenda. Both of these effects increase transaction costs. Corruption also gives organizations an alternative way to maximize profits. If government officials can be bought, then a firm can gain an unfair market advantage.

The prevalence of corruption is primarily a function of its perceived costs and benefits. Other things being equal, the greater the reward and the lower the chances of being caught and punished, the more likely it is that people will engage in corrupt activities. To limit corruption, the institutional framework must reduce potential gains from illegal government activity, raise the probability of detection, and make prosecution and other sanctions a real threat.[15] We deal with each of these in turn.

The potential for gain from corruption arises when a government official has the authority to set policy or to ration resources to favor one group at the expense of another. For example, if the government makes available a limited amount of subsidies to the poor, then the person in charge of the funds can allocate them on the basis of who pays the highest kickback. If a trade official sets tariff rates, then the rates may be based on industry payments to the official. And as the recent events in the Asian economies have shown, if government controls the allocation of credit, either directly or indirectly, then credit may flow to the president's friends instead of flowing to the most deserving recipients. The best way to reduce the gains from corruption is to reduce the discretion government officials have over funds and policies. This means standardizing policies and allowing the market to allocate resources when it makes sense to do so. If, for example, loans are made by the private sector on the basis of a competitive market process, then the opportunity for bribery is reduced. If the rules for tariffs are relatively simple and understood by all, then the ability of the trade official to extract revenue is dampened, because people clearly understand that they are being taken advantage of.

The payoff to corruption can also be limited by raising the costs of engaging in corruption. In part this means making it more likely that those engaging in corruption will be detected. Freedom of the press is important for monitoring the state's actions. If the press can easily monitor the behavior of government officials, then at least the government official must be more discrete in engaging in corrupt activities. A system of checks and balances is also essential. In the United States there are several governmental agencies that supervise commercial banks.[16] This overlapping of jurisdiction gives banks alternatives if one regulatory agency is abusing its powers. As another example, collection of customs duties could be handled by a few different agencies, making it less likely that any given agency will embezzle funds. Anonymous whistle-blowing laws are also important in order for ordinary citizens to report corruption.

The third component to limiting corruption is the possibility of prosecution. Judicial independence is a primary avenue for raising the probability of prosecution from engagement in corrupt activities.[17] Judicial independence requires a set of formal institutions guaranteeing the judicial system the final word in legislative activity and enforcement. In this environment, the legislative and executive branches of government are ultimately held accountable for their actions. If corruption is detected, the judicial system can impose the necessary penalties on the guilty parties. Judges must be personally insulated from the consequences of their decisions. If, for example, the legislative or executive branch influences the employment status or the physical safety of judges, then the integrity of the system is questioned. Judges must have long-term tenure to provide freedom to act as they see fit. In many nations the executive branch is considered to be above the law, and hence the judicial system has no ultimate authority over the executive's actions. In this environment, the effectiveness of the judicial system in limiting corruption is diminished.

The perceived costs and benefits from engaging in corruption explain much of the prevalence or absence of corruption in a given nation. But corruption is not only a function of the costs and benefits; informal institutions play a large role as well. If a nation has a history of corruption, and children are raised seeing corrupt activities as normal and accepted, then those children are more likely to permit corruption as adults. If the values of many citizens are such that they abhor corruption, however, then corruption will be limited. For a nation with high levels of corruption, it may be necessary to prosecute offenders severely until corruption is diminished and informal institutions change over time.

The state creates most of the formal institutions of a nation. In order to produce efficient institutions, the polity must be organized in such a way that markets are encouraged and protected. Moreover, institutions must exist to minimize corruption. Market-preserving federalism is one type of political system that allows markets to prosper by fostering competition for economic organizations at the subnational level. For the formal rules of a nation to be respected, corruption must be limited. This can be achieved by increasing the likelihood of detection, by punishing more severely the transgressors, and by reducing the opportunity for individuals in the government to engage in corruption. An economy can perform well only if markets are protected and corruption is limited; therefore, political reorganization is usually a necessary condition for strong economic growth.

Questions for Discussion

1. What is the role of the constitution in a nation? Is a constitution necessary and/or sufficient for good economic performance?

2. Imagine that the president of the United States dismissed the House and the Senate. How would you react? If the abolition of Congress succeeded, what impact would this have on U.S. economic performance?

3. Why is it that, other things being equal, a heterogeneous and diverse society is less likely to be able to limit the power of government? Give some historical examples of this situation.

4. Suppose that capital and labor mobility were severely limited because of relocation restrictions across subnational jurisdictions. Would the political system produce market-preserving, efficient institutions? Explain.

5. Name one nation that has relatively little corruption and one nation in which corruption and bribery are common. Draw from your personal experience if possible. What explains the difference in the level of corruption between these countries?

Notes

1. Barry R. Weingast, "The Economic Role of Political Institutions: Market-Preserving Federalism and Economic Development," *Journal of Law, Economics, and Organization*, vol. 11, no. 1 (1995), p. 1.

2. Douglass C. North, *Structure and Change in Economic History* (New York: W. W. Norton, 1981), p. 21.

3. This is analogous to the common microeconomic assumption that firms act in such a way as to maximize profits. Most firms do not have profit maximization as their only goal, but it is a common enough goal that this assumption allows us to explain a great deal of firm behavior. Likewise, not all rulers acted to maximize their personal wealth, but it was a common enough motive that it allows us to explain a great deal of behavior.

4. A discriminating monopolist is able to charge different prices for the product on the basis of the elasticity of demand. The more inelastic the demand for the good, the higher the price the monopolist will charge. For example, airlines behave somewhat like discriminating monopolists when they segregate the market into business and leisure travelers.

5. *Wall Street Journal* and Heritage Foundation, *1997 Index of Economic Freedom*, ed. Kim R. Holmes, Bryan T. Johnson, and Melanie Kirkpatrick, p. 7.

6. *The Economist*, "Democracy and Growth: Why Voting Is Good for You," August 27, 1994, p. 15.

7. Ibid., p. 16.

8. Ibid., p. 17.

9. Douglass C. North, "A Transaction Cost Theory of Politics," *Journal of Theoretical Politics*, vol. 2, no. 4 (1990), p. 360.

10. Barry R. Weingast and W. J. Marshall, "The Industrial Organization of Congress; or, Why Legislatures, Like Firms, Are Not Organized as Markets," *Journal of Political Economy*, vol. 96 (1988), pp. 132–163.

11. Weingast, "The Economic Role of Political Institutions," p. 4. This section on federalism draws heavily on Weingast's article.

12. Ibid.

13. Indeed, we have observed this phenomenon. Some insurance companies, for example, stopped selling insurance in the state of California after the state placed price ceilings and minimum-quality constraints on the policies being offered there.

14. Weingast, "The Economic Role of Political Institutions," p. 10.

15. World Bank, *World Development Report*, "Restraining Arbitrary State Action and Corruption," 1997, p. 105.

16. These are the Comptroller of the Currency, the Federal Deposit Insurance Corporation (FDIC), and the Federal Reserve. Each state also regulates banks in its jurisdiction.

17. *World Development Report*, 1997, p. 100.

7

Transition from Socialism
to Capitalism

The usefulness of any economic theory lies in its ability to explain real-world events accurately and to serve as a policy guide for enhancing economic performance. The theory of institutions laid out in the previous chapters can be applied to a broad range of events. This chapter applies the New Institutional Economics to transition economies and explains the necessary reconstruction of institutions that must take place in order for the transition to be successful. It examines the experience of East Germany in the reunification with West Germany and describes the key microeconomic and macroeconomic issues that transition economies face. The prognosis for many transition economies is unclear. As explained earlier, an economy may not be able to institute the necessary changes even if it knows what to do. It is much easier for a doctor to prescribe treatment than to force the patient to follow it, and often the doctor does not even know the correct treatment to prescribe.

East Germany Versus West Germany

Economic history has given us something of a natural experiment on the impact of socialist versus capitalist institutions on economic performance. A good case study would be a comparison of economic performance in East and West Germany from 1945 to 1989.[1] Before World War II Germany was a unified nation. The people of what was to become East and West Germany had a similar culture and religion and similar life experiences. The fundamental difference after 1945 was that East Germany remained under the control of the Soviet Union and adopted socialist institutions while West Germany was reconstructed under democratic, capitalistic institutions.

Table 7.1 lists key comparative economic statistics for the year 1988. The difference in living standards in just a forty-five-year period is striking: GDP per capita was three times higher in the West. Even this statistic understates the true difference in living standards, because a smaller percentage of production in the East was for domestic consumption. Perhaps more telling is that those in the East had to work six times as long as those in the West to purchase a shirt, and twelve times as long to purchase a color television set.

Socialism is a type of economic system that relies on government planning to ration scarce resources and to coordinate market activity. Every nation must address three economic questions. First, what will be produced? Because human needs and desires exceed limited resources, we must ration those resources in some manner. Socialist economies ration resources by detailed government planning. Heads of industries meet with government officials annually to decide what goods and services are to be produced. The former Soviet Union and many other socialist nations developed elaborate five-year plans in which they prioritized production of particular quantities of goods and services, and then rationed the necessary resources to produce the amount specified in the plan. If a good was deemed a low-priority item, its production received little or no resources. Because industry and defense received higher priority than consumer products and agriculture, citizens of the Soviet Union had relatively low consumption levels. Capitalist economies, in contrast, ration scarce resources mainly on the basis of consumer demand. Private firms produce those goods and services that consumers demand. When a particular product becomes more popular, the price usually rises, and more resources are diverted into the production of that item.

The second question that all economies must answer is how to produce the goods and services. In socialist systems, managers and government officials plan the production process and the technology used. Individual plants may have some leeway to influence the production process, but as

TABLE 7.1   Key Comparative Economic Statistics, West and East Germany, 1988

	West Germany	East Germany
Household income (DM/M)	3,850	1,270
Household financial assets	1,196.6	167.2
Work hours required for a:		
Man's shirt	1.22	7.19
Color television set	81.34	1,008.56

SOURCES: Income and assets: Paul R. Gregory and Robert C. Stuart, *Comparative Economic Systems*, 5th ed. (Boston: Houghton Mifflin, 1995), p. 221. Work hours: J. Barkley Rosser Jr. and Marina V. Rosser, *Comparative Economics in a Transforming World Economy* (Chicago: Irwin, 1996), p. 219.

discussed later, there is little incentive to do so. Capitalist economies leave to private firms the decision of how to produce. In theory, firms produce in such a way as to minimize their costs of production. If machinery is relatively expensive, firms use more labor. Government may set some regulations on the production process, imposing environmental regulations, for example, but firms still have much leeway in deciding how to produce their products.

The third question is, for whom are the goods and services produced? Socialist economies answer this in two ways. First, the government determines employee wages. The wages determine income and hence consumption levels. Second, the government directly sets the prices for goods and services. In theory, a socialist government could set prices so that supply equals demand. If there are long lines for certain products, the price could be increased until the lines disappear. In practice, however, long lines are commonplace, because governments keep the prices of key products low for political and social reasons. Typically, energy and food staples are priced at a fraction of their production costs. Therefore, many goods are produced for those who are able and willing to wait in long lines. In the Soviet Union, for example, bread prices were unchanged for thirty years. Bread was so cheap that "peasants found it advantageous to feed bread rather than grain to their livestock."[2] Market economies also produce the goods and services for those who have income. However, income is not set directly by the government.[3] Wages, like most prices, are set by the forces of supply and demand. One consequence of this is that capitalist economies tend to have more income inequality than socialist economies. West Germany, for example, had more income inequality than East Germany even though average income levels in West Germany were much higher.

After World War II, East Germany adopted Stalinist reforms calling for central planning and promotion of large state-owned enterprises. Private ownership was forbidden, and assets were seized by the state. Firms had no influence in setting prices, and wages were determined by the state. Initially, East German economic performance was fairly decent; growth rates were high. Recall from the production possibilities frontier that economic growth can result from movement from an inefficient point inside the frontier to an efficient point on the frontier, from an increase in the resource base (extensive growth), or from an increase in technology (intensive growth). East Germany primarily took advantage of exploitation of untapped resources and economies of scale, which resulted in extensive growth. No doubt there were large inefficiencies in resource allocation, demonstrated by long lines and frequent shortages of key consumer goods. However, for a while growth could occur because more resources were mobilized. Labor force participation rates for women increased dramatically, as did the average number of hours worked per week. Natural resources were used in the extension of East Germany's industries. Moreover, income inequality was low, and the unemployment rate was nearly zero.[4] However, the good economic performance began to slow dramatically in the 1960s, and the economy stagnated. The gap between the West and the East increased. Why did this happen?

Recall from our static model that there are several necessary conditions that must be present to allow markets to function well, including good consumer information, a stable monetary system, secure property rights over the product both before and after the sale, and access to a third-party system to enforce transactions. Socialist economies satisfied these criteria. Given that there was little or no choice in product selection, consumer information was not very important. East Germany had a stable monetary system, and property rights were specified and enforced by the state. Strict enforcement mechanisms were in place to oppress reactionaries. The result was that costs of transacting were low.[5]

Chapter 4 argued that low transaction costs should allow for good economic performance. If transaction costs were low, why was the performance of East Germany so dismal relative to West Germany? The answer is that *dynamic incentives were absent.* Recall that for intensive growth to occur, institutions must foster the process of creative destruction in which new technology destroys the old. This requires supply-side competition and profit-seeking behavior. Socialist economies, by their very nature, do not promote competition. Proper dynamic incentives also require capital markets that respond to the potential for earning a return, not to the whims of state bureaucrats. In socialist economies, funds were rationed on the basis of how they had been rationed the previous year and of who was the most influential in the political process. There was no concern for channeling funds to investments with big potential returns. East German workers, in contrast to their counterparts in the West, had no incentive to improve the products that they produced. Even if the technology reduced production costs, the employees did not receive higher wages. Quality-enhancing technology was also unimportant, because prices were set by the state and consumer demand was guaranteed. Consumers had to buy the inferior product, since there were no alternatives available. Moreover, if a firm found a way to produce the output quota using fewer resources, then the quantity of resources allotted to the firm the following year may have fallen. These incentives are analogous to a government agency that must spend all of its budget in a given year even if it does not need all of the funds, in order to avoid cuts during the following year. For these reasons, dynamic incentives were absent and technology lagged behind, along with productivity and wealth.

The failure to improve technology was not uniform across all areas in socialist economies. Recall that the Soviet Union and the United States fought a Cold War for more than four decades. It was never clear during that time who had the superior defense technology. The perception was that Soviet defense technology kept pace with U.S. defense technology. There was intensive growth in this area because the socialist states were in competition with the Western world. The defense industry received the brightest workers and significant state resources. The Soviet Union spent a far greater percentage of its resources on defense even compared to the United States. The Soviet Union and East Germany also excelled in international Olympic competition. They treated the Olympics with a degree of paranoia to the extent that new rules had to be devised by the Olympic committee over who could qualify as a woman athlete, because some female competitors from these countries had significant male characteristics. But these examples were the exception rather than the rule. Most sectors had low productivity growth because of the inability to develop and integrate new technology into their production processes. As a consequence, living standards in the socialist economies fell far behind those in the West.

The Merger

In the late 1980s the disintegration of socialist economies began in earnest. The Berlin Wall was torn down November 9, 1989. Poland, Hungary, and Czechoslovakia (now the countries of the Czech Republic and Slovakia) cast off socialism in peaceful elections. The process culminated in the disintegration of the Soviet Union on December 25, 1991. In essence the political, economic, and social institutions that had held these socialist economies together crumbled. Economies can be dismantled much easier than they can be put back together, but reconstruction is exactly what the former socialist economies must do. The key to a successful transition to capitalism is to create an institutional framework that provides low costs of transacting and dynamic incentives for technological progress.

In which of these four countries do you suspect that transition is proceeding the smoothest: Russia, Poland, the former East Germany, or the Czech Republic? The answer is East Germany.[6] Why? With reunification in place, East Germany dissolved its socialist institutions and adopted those of West Germany. Eastern Germany instantly had access to western Germany's property rights and its system of enforcement. Eastern Germany had access to a stable currency, well-functioning capital markets, democratic political institutions, and a social safety net to take care of those in need. East Germany was unique in that it was the only former socialist economy that did not have to rebuild these institutions from the ground up. As such, East Germany made the transition from socialism to capitalism with the least difficulty of all the former socialist economies. The main steps that had to be taken were to liberalize prices and to privatize assets.

This does not mean that there were no problems with the transition. Indeed, Germany is still going through difficult adjustments more than seven years after the transition. Germany had to address two issues immediately: currency integration and privatization of eastern German assets. Western Germany agreed to exchange East German marks at a rate of one to one, despite the fact that the East German mark was worth only a fraction of the West German mark. The agreement was more for political reasons than economic considerations. The one-to-one exchange had two consequences. First, those converting East German marks into West German marks received a large increase in purchasing power. Second, the cost of conversion to western Germany was much more expensive. Since many wages and welfare payments were tied to the currency valuation, real wages and subsidies paid to former East German citizens increased dramatically. This led to an unusually large budget deficit and higher taxes in order to absorb the costs of unification. The inflation rate in West Germany has been one of the lowest in the world in the post–World War II era, rarely exceeding 2 percent. However, unification costs and the subsequent expansion of the money supply pushed inflation above 6 percent in 1992.[7] Moreover, there was a possibility that Germany's budget deficit in 1997 would exceed the standards that Germany itself helped to prescribe for entry into the Euro-currency system.[8] However, by sharply raising taxes, Germany managed to reduce its deficit-to-GDP ratio under the 3 percent limit to 2.7 percent in 1997.[9]

Privatization of eastern German assets was accomplished through the Treuhandstalt agency, the organization responsible for selling former state-owned enterprises. The Treuhandstalt agency generally broke up pieces of existing firms and looked for buyers, most of whom came from western Germany. Those firms that could not be sold were liquidated.

During the transition, output in eastern Germany collapsed. There were a variety of reasons for this, but the simple explanation is that eastern Germany produced noncompetitive, low-quality products that few wished to purchase. Eastern Germans flocked to the West in order to purchase the higher-quality products. Moreover, the one-to-one currency exchange resulted in wages in eastern firms comparable to those in the West. The problem was that productivity in eastern Germany was much lower, and therefore real wages were much higher, making production costs in eastern Germany prohibitively high. With the output collapse came a surge in unemployment in the east. Unofficially, it was estimated that one in three workers lost their jobs, though the official unemployment rate peaked at 16.5 percent in 1992.[10] Unemployment in the East has remained stubbornly high. In 1996 unemployment in eastern Germany was 15.7 percent, and the rate in western Germany was 9.1 percent. As late as February 1998, total German unemployment was 12.6 percent, but unemployment in western Germany was significantly lower at 10.4 percent. The poor employment performance comes in spite of massive government transfers. "Since 1990 the German government in Bonn has given more than $600 billion to its former eastern rival through business subsidies, special tax breaks, and support payments for individuals. . . . [C]ompanies have invested $500 billion more."[11]

Despite the hardships involved with Germany's unification, it has been a relatively easy process compared to all the other transition economies. There is no serious potential for revolution in Germany, the democratic system is not threatened, inflation remains low and the currency stable, a generous social safety net is in place, and there is opportunity and hope for many of the eastern German citizens who can learn the skills needed to function in a market economy. In short, the East German transition was relatively easy because the nation was able to adopt the political, social, and economic institutions of West Germany.

In making the transition from socialism, there are critical macroeconomic and microeconomic issues to consider. The macroeconomic issues generally have to do with price and business-cycle stability, and the microeconomic issues involve the reconstructing of the market system. The macroeconomic and microeconomic issues complement one another, and both are necessary for a successful transition. We deal with the macroeconomic issues first.

Macroeconomic Issues

The ultimate goal of macroeconomic policy is to create an environment in which people do not have to be overly concerned about sharp output fluctuations and the inflation and currency risks of making exchanges over time. This type of environment lowers transaction costs and facilitates growth. There are five key issues at the macroeconomic level that a transition government must address. It must control inflation, reduce the budget deficit to a reasonable level, stabilize the value of the currency, open its economy to foreign trade, and attract investment to generate economic growth.

One of the first steps in constructing market economies is to abolish price controls set by the government and let prices float in the market. Price liberalization touches off an initial burst of price increases because many basic goods and services were purposely underpriced. Moreover, the supply shortage in socialist nations leads to *monetary overhang*, a situation in which there is ample currency in the economy but few goods and services to purchase. Price liberalization leads to sharply rising prices as large sums of currency compete for the limited supply of goods. The government must convince its citizens that the price liberalization is a one-time price shock, and prices will not rise so quickly in the near future. If not, the inflation can be built into people's expectations and quickly turn into a wage-price spiral. When an economy experiences hyperinflation, transaction costs become extremely high. The monetary system, whose function is to facilitate exchanges by eliminating the need for a double coincidence of wants, becomes increasingly irrelevant. It is difficult for economic growth to occur in this environment.

Closely tied to inflation is the size of the budget deficit. The budget deficit is the difference between government outlays and tax revenues. During transition, tax revenues decrease along with production, and the need for government spending generally increases or at least decreases by a smaller amount than tax revenue. This leads to larger deficits. Two budget priorities in particular strain the budget. First, socialist governments directly provide operating funds to state-owned enterprises (SOEs). For political, economic, and social reasons, governments are reluctant to reduce or eliminate this funding. To do so means that employees are laid off, potential voters become angry, and poverty and homelessness increase. Hence SOEs continue to operate despite large losses. Even if the SOEs are semiprivate after the transition, they often operate under what is called a *soft budget constraint*, in which the government is the underlying source of funding if an organization has a negative net income. There is no need to change organizational behavior to cut losses or make a profit, because the firm knows that the government will make up the loss. Second, the social safety net must expand to take care of the newly unemployed and the expanding poor class. This entails additional government spending for social programs.

These budget priorities occur in the context of falling tax revenues. Tax collection poses a severe problem for former socialist economies. Under socialism, the state simply kept the profits from its enterprises. There was no need for an income tax, as the state determined workers' wages directly. An income tax would have been redundant, with the government giving the workers wages and then recollecting a percentage of the income in tax revenue. Now with firms in private hands and employers free to set wages, incomes are not determined by the government. Most Western economies use an income tax to extract resources from the private sector. An income tax system requires accurate recording of workers' incomes, tax laws to specify tax levels, and an enforcement agency to collect taxes. The agency must have the power to detect and punish tax avoiders. So the tax system runs on an elaborate set of formal rules and enforcement. Perhaps the most important aspect of whether or not a tax system works is societal attitude toward taxes. Even in the United States, the tax system primarily works because people voluntarily participate. If a nation's citizens think that taxes are for the most part fairly assessed and collected and are necessary to fund legitimate government operations, most will pay taxes willingly even as they grumble. If the citizens feel that taxes are unfair and are not sure where the tax revenues go, they will not pay them. Any government has only a limited amount of resources to spend on monitoring and detecting tax avoiders, so most will get away with not paying taxes. West Germany had a tax system and enforcement mechanisms already set up that eastern Germany simply adopted; the other countries had to build such a system. The rise in expenditures combined with the fall in taxes leads to budget pressures. If the government cannot pay its debts with existing tax revenue, it may print money in order to pay off debts. This often leads to hyperinflation. The solution is to cut subsidies to SOEs, reduce other nonessential expenditures, and create an effective tax system. While economically expedient, these prescriptions are often politically impossible for transition economies to accomplish.

A third macroeconomic issue is the stability of the value of the currency on international markets. This typically requires a large initial devaluation because of past government support of an overvalued currency. But downward pressure on the currency continues even after the initial devaluation, because inflation makes the domestic currency less valuable, but also because exports fall with the transition and the collapse of the socialist trading blocks. Moreover, the new consumer freedom leads to a surge in imports. The ensuing trade deficit results in more foreign exchange being demanded by the transition economy than supplied; hence devaluation occurs. Measures that restrict imports can ease downward pressure on the currency in the short term, but long-term success requires a healthy and growing export sector.

Transition economies must choose the type of exchange rate policy that they wish to follow. There are at least three possibilities. First, the nation could follow a fixed exchange rate policy in which the value of the domestic currency is tied to a foreign currency (or a "basket" of currencies) whose value is stable. This allows the exchange rate to serve as an anchor for inflation expectations. If the value of the Polish zloty, for example, is tied to the U.S. dollar, then to avoid devaluation, the rate of inflation in the Polish economy must be similar to that in the United States. If Polish inflation rates continually surpass those of the United States, then devaluation is inevitable. Therefore, a fixed exchange rate provides the economy with a measure of inflation expectations in controlling inflation.[12]

The opposite extreme is a flexible exchange rate policy. In this case market forces determine the international value of the currency. The advantage of this system is that monetary policy can be conducted with less regard for effects on the currency. Moreover, the exchange rate adjusts to keep exports competitive and trade deficits at reasonable levels. But the opportunity cost is the chance to reduce inflation more aggressively, because there is no foreign currency to serve as an anchor for inflation. Reliance on the market also leads to highly variable exchange rates in the short run, increasing exchange rate risk and making foreign transactions more difficult.[13]

In the third possibility, which is a compromise between the two extreme policies, the government fixes the exchange rate at a certain level and then gradually devalues the currency on the basis of a preannounced schedule. This exchange rate policy is called a *crawling peg*. It is an adaptation of a fixed exchange rate policy in an environment in which domestic inflation exceeds the inflation rate of the country to whose currency the exchange rate is tied. This has the advantage of serving as a moving anchor for inflation expectations, and it is more realistic in situations in which inflation cannot be brought to, say, 2 or 3 percent per year. Thus the government does not place itself in a position in which it will lose its inflation-fighting credibility after one currency devaluation.

The fourth key macroeconomic transition issue is to stimulate foreign trade. This calls for the elimination of foreign-exchange restrictions that limit the buying and selling of foreign exchange. The socialist governments typically had currencies that were not tradable on the open market. Only certain government agencies had direct access to foreign currency. Such a situation is not sustainable in an environment in which businesses must export and import large volumes of goods and services. Selected access to foreign exchange opens the door for political corruption as firms exchange profits and other privileges for access to foreign exchange markets. Exchange-rate controls also hinder business people and tourists from traveling abroad. Such controls must be eliminated. Tariffs and quotas must also be reduced in order to stimulate foreign trade. This is necessary to be able to import needed goods and services, and to force the country to focus on its comparative advantage in production. As Latin America has demonstrated, a high level of protection leads to inefficient capitalist organizations and inhibits economic growth in the long run.

Finally, the government must attract foreign investment. Foreign investment provides at least two benefits for the recipient economy. First, it provides needed capital, technology, and management expertise. Since transition economies typically have low levels of saving and need to play catch-up in the technology game, foreign investment becomes particularly important. Second, it helps to ease the pressure on the exchange rate. Devaluation pressures result from excess demand of foreign currencies over the domestic currency. When foreign firms or governments invest in a transition economy, demand for the domestic currency rises, reducing pressures for devaluation. In general, transition economies have done a poor job at attracting foreign investment. Hungary leads the pack by far in attracting foreign investment. Between 1989 and 1995, Hungary attracted over $10.6 billion, which accounts for 30 percent of its 1994 GDP.[14] Estonia is second, attracting nearly 15 percent of its 1994 GDP in foreign investment, followed closely by the Czech Republic. Foreign investors want essentially the same thing they desire in their host country. They desire secure property rights, macroeconomic stability, and an institutional framework that treats foreign firms fairly. Transition economies have often had a hard time delivering these things.

There is a debate as to whether or not macroeconomic stabilization is necessary for economic growth. *Stabilization policies* are macroeconomic policies aimed at reducing inflation by reducing the budget deficit and devaluing the currency. Many lending agencies such as the International Monetary Fund (IMF) require that countries undergo stabilization before any funds will be lent to the country. However, these stabilization policies are painful. They require cuts in expenditures and increases in taxes at a time when many citizens are reeling from the chaos of transition. In other words, the medicine seems to dole out more pain. Is stabilization necessary for economic growth? A recent study suggests that it is. Stanley Fischer and his colleagues compared the economic performance of transition economies and found that "low inflation—below 50 percent in annual terms—is a necessary condition for growth to begin."[15] Generally speaking, growth begins to occur two years after effective stabilization programs are implemented. Those countries that have yet to stabilize are experiencing dismal economic performance. This result should not be surprising. A main theme of this book is that low transaction costs is a prerequisite for good economic performance. A stable macroeconomic environment is essential for facilitating transactions.

Microeconomic Issues

Transition economies also face key microeconomic issues. The ultimate goal is to replace the planning system with a well-functioning, efficient market system backed by an institutional framework that allows low-cost transactions. The process involves price liberalization, privatization, the development of capital markets, and the creation of a legal system that specifies and enforces property rights, establishes contract law, and promotes competition. We deal with each of these in turn.

Price liberalization is perhaps the easiest to accomplish, since it involves removing controls rather than imposing new ones. Price liberalization has at least three advantages. First, it reduces the inefficiencies involved in resource allocation. Resources are priced closer to their opportunity cost. Second, the government eliminates or reduces subsidies on many products, which in turn reduces its budget deficit. Third, price flexibility (combined with privatization) allows the profit motive to operate if other supply conditions are present. Firms can set prices in order to maximize profits. But even in this area there are many difficulties. When prices adjust to their market values, goods and services that were subsidized by the state become very expensive. Such a price adjustment, given fixed or declining incomes, can lead to starvation and death. Energy use, for example, is so pervasive that everyone in the economy is affected by its price. The Soviet Union heavily subsidized energy prices. An instantaneous price release in Russia would have sent devastating shock waves through the economy, and many Russians would have had to face the winters with little or no heat. So Russia opted for a more gradual increase in energy prices. Over the longer term energy prices can be liberalized, but incomes must rise and social safety nets should be in place in order to limit the harmful impact.

The second microeconomic issue is privatization. Private ownership of property is essential in providing solid dynamic incentives for profit-maximizing behavior. Individuals must be assured that they will earn a return on their capital and labor; otherwise they have little reason to invest in businesses or to create new businesses. With secure property rights, people are more willing to work hard to succeed. But the process of privatization has not been easy for transition economies. There are a variety of ways to privatize, each with different consequences for income distribution. The most common methods of privatization are restitution processes, sale of state property, mass voucher systems, and formation of new privately owned enterprises.[16]

Restitution involves transferring assets, particularly land, to their original, pre-socialism owners. This process is fraught with difficulty, as records are incomplete and property rights are in dispute. Moreover, many of the legitimate owners of agricultural land, for example, left the farm years ago and know nothing about farming. But restitution laws often require them to farm the land they receive. Returning the land to its original owners in this manner is inefficient. Restitution has also been applied to apartments and housing units. The problem in this case is to dislodge the current tenants.

The sale of state property is a way for the government to rid itself of budget-draining enterprises and to encourage private ownership. One difficulty in selling SOEs, however, is that many large industrial firms are old and inefficient, unable to compete in a more open economy. It is difficult to price such assets accurately. Therefore, many state assets are sitting idle or are continuing to operate at heavy losses. Furthermore, as noted earlier, it is difficult politically to sell off SOEs. Such action leads to unemployment and angry voters.

A *voucher system* has been used extensively by many of the transition governments. Under this plan, governments issue vouchers to all citizens, and the vouchers can be sold or used to purchase shares of assets. This has the advantage of distributing resources equitably, but it dilutes the ownership of assets such that managers and workers of firms may have no more control over their firms than anyone else. To circumvent this, Russia has allowed employees and management to purchase up to half of their own firms first before general vouchers can be used. Hungary has resisted a voucher system and has privatized by selling off firms for cash, often to foreign investors.

Another privatization avenue, finally, is the formation of new enterprises. This is perhaps the most important process over the long term. Poland is generally regarded as having the most dynamic small-business sector.[17] Most of the privatization has proceeded very slowly in the transforming countries. By the end of 1994 only the Czech Republic had a share of GDP generated by the private sector that exceeded 55 percent. Poland, Hungary, Estonia, Latvia, Lithuania, and Russia had private shares between 50 percent and 55 percent. All the remaining transition economies had percentages below this level. Most of the former Soviet republics are having a particularly difficult time in efforts to privatize.

The third major microeconomic issue is the creation of capital markets—that is, the creation of institutions and organizations that facilitate the process of lending and borrowing. These markets are critical, because economic growth depends on the levels of saving and investment. Those who need the investment funds are not always the ones who have the funds. If capital markets work poorly, investment and economic growth are significantly reduced, because potential investment opportunities are forfeited. The economy lags behind others who are able to channel the funds to their most efficient uses.

The exchange process of borrowing and lending money (especially in large amounts) is plagued with inherently high transaction costs. Measurement costs are high because the lender typically has very poor information as to how the funds are being used by the borrower. It is time-consuming to monitor how others are performing their jobs, particularly when the lender is located some distance from the borrower. There is also an ever-present risk of default. In most countries there is a limit to how strict the enforcement institutions can be. Most countries have eliminated debtor's prisons, and debtors are given partial escape clauses through bankruptcy laws. This makes enforcement costs much higher. Although institutions cannot eliminate these measurement and enforcement costs, they can significantly reduce them. In the United States this has been accomplished in the banking system by the creation of deposit insurance and a whole network of bank supervisors and regulators. The stock market is regulated just as tightly. The Securities and Exchange Commission (SEC) is responsible for regulating firms' access to the stock market and ensuring that firms that sell shares disclose their financial condition accurately to the public.

Socialist capital markets were relatively simple. In general, there was one central bank in each country. The bank was responsible for holding deposits for customers, circulating the currency in the economy, and lending funds to SOEs in amounts predetermined by government planning. There was no competition for deposits, and bankers did not have to make decisions about where the limited funds were to be lent. The risk of default was low, since the revenue of the firm was fairly certain, and if default was imminent, the government could easily intervene to bail the firm out. After all, the government would not let the state bank fail. Despite the low transaction costs in this system, resource allocation of the scarce funds was not based on potential returns, but on government decisions. Funds were not channeled to the firms that had the ideas to develop new products, but to those that had received funds the year before. There was no facilitation of Schumpeter's process of creative destruction; instead there was a reinforcement of the status quo.

Transition calls for a completely different type of banking system. In capitalist economies, numerous banks compete for deposits and then make (often risky) decisions about how to allocate those funds. The monetary system is controlled by a central bank whose job it is to make sure that the financial system operates smoothly. In this environment, funds are channeled to those who can convince the banks that they will earn returns high enough to pay back the bank with interest. Along the way, many of those firms will produce new products or develop new technologies that lead to higher standards of living. Transition to capitalism means that former socialist countries must redefine the role of their central banks, foster competition in the banking system, and create institutions and organizations that regulate and supervise the behavior of the newly emerging banks to reduce the depositors' risk.

Stock and bond markets also must be created. As pervasive as banks are in the United States, they account for only around 6 percent of all credit flows in the economy. Stock and bond markets are useful for very large transactions. Setting up a stock exchange is not very difficult, but getting it to perform well is extremely difficult. In fact, many developing nations have either very small stock markets or none at all. A well-functioning stock exchange requires detailed and refined institutional structure to define property rights and to monitor and enforce exchanges. But if transition economies wish to become full participants in market economies, they must create stock markets—and this takes time and institutional evolution. Thus far stock markets in transition economies are small and illiquid. The Czech Republic has the largest exchange relative to the size of its economy, but the turnover tends to be low.[18] Bond markets typically precede and complement stock markets. Bond markets are more secure, because there is a legal obligation for the debtor to repay the creditor. Governments often instigate or facilitate the creation of bond markets. The U.S. government, for example, typically borrows over US$100 billion annually in the bond market. This has helped to stimulate a sophisticated secondary market for government bonds. Creation of capital markets in transition economies will take time. But they are essential for facilitating the saving and investment process in capitalist economies.

The fourth key microeconomic issue is the development of a legal system that specifies and enforces property rights, establishes contract law, and promotes competition. This task is at the heart of constructing the institutional framework vital to lowering transaction costs and creating a dynamic market economy. Specification of property rights goes beyond the initial phases of privatization. Rights concerning inventory, lease arrangements, intellectual property, and so on must be specified as clearly as possible. Protection of intellectual property rights is a big concern for many foreign businesses. Without these rights, firms could steal the technology embedded in foreign products. But if ownership rights are clear and enforcement mechanisms are present, then uncertainty in transactions diminishes. When goods and services are exchanged, disputes and disagreements arise frequently. Contract law is necessary to limit and resolve these disputes. Good contract law is evolutionary; it evolves as markets do. It requires dynamic legislation and enforcement by government agencies or the judicial branch. Transaction costs are dramatically higher without a reliable method for resolving contract disputes.

Transition governments must promote competition. They face the challenge of demonopolizing their SOEs. The process of creative destruction requires a competitive economy in which organizations battle one another for supremacy. But Stalinist socialist economies were based on large industrial enterprises designed to fully exploit economies of scale.

Not only was competition eliminated, it was looked down upon as one of the pitfalls of capitalism. The privatization process is crucial to de-monopolization. In the process of privatization, large state firms can be broken into multiple parts. Moreover, new firms should be encouraged to compete against the existing state firms. The problem is that the large existing firms have customer bases, name recognition, and cost advantages because of economies of scale. New firms must be able to compete in this environment. The state must also adopt institutions that promote competition. Antitrust laws that prevent certain mergers and other non-competitive organizational behavior must be developed and enforced. Antitrust laws are complex. There is a fine balance to be struck between competitive and noncompetitive behavior. For example, if a firm is so successful that it drives out its major competitors, should this be punished or rewarded? As is the case in the United States, common law must develop to interpret and enforce the details of antitrust laws.

Entry and exit institutions also must be specified. Freedom of entry and exit are essential in creating competitive and efficient markets. Firms must be able to enter industries with minimal rules and regulations. Exit laws include bankruptcy laws to allow for the orderly dissolution of failed businesses or the reorganization of temporarily illiquid ones.

Unfortunately, as we shall see in our analysis of Russia, these initial steps of price liberalization, privatization, the establishment of capital markets, and establishing a legal framework are only the beginning of the process of generating efficient market systems. These are difficult processes that can take decades to accomplish.

The issues discussed here refer only to formal institutions and enforcement mechanisms. Informal rules must adapt as well if transaction costs are to be lowered. Many perceive the rationing of goods and services on the basis of market forces as unfair. When there is a shortage of bread, should prices rise or should those who need bread simply wait in line longer? If a significant number of a nation's citizens do not perceive the rules of the game to be fair, transition will be slow and difficult. Moreover, it is much easier to write new rules and regulations than it is to persuade people to enforce the rules. How can a government ensure that its judges will act fairly? How can we guarantee that those in power will serve the people and not simply use the power for their own gain? In fact we cannot guarantee these things. So much of any economy's performance depends on its informal institutions, which change very slowly. Thus even if all the formal rules are put into place, a transition economy may still endure poor economic performance.

We have much to learn from the experiences of the countries that have undertaken the transition to capitalism. We now turn our focus to an analysis of transition in Poland and Russia.

Questions for Discussion

1. Discuss the reasons why the transition of East Germany has been easier than the transition in all other former socialist economies.
2. Macroeconomic adjustment and stabilization seems to cause much pain and suffering, especially among the poor. Is there a way to avoid this? If not, is the macroeconomic adjustment worth the pain?
3. Microeconomic reform involves price liberalization and privatization. Which of these should be done first? Why? Are these two steps sufficient to promote good economic performance? Explain.
4. Discuss the advantages and disadvantages of fixed, flexible, and crawling peg exchange rate policies.
5. In March 1998 the IMF soundly rejected Indonesia's plan for a fixed exchange rate. Why do you think it did so?

Notes

1. North Korea and South Korea are also appropriate for such a comparison in the years following the Korean War.

2. Marshall I. Goldman, *Lost Opportunity: Why Economic Reforms in Russia Have Not Worked* (New York: W. W. Norton, 1994), p. 99.

3. The major exception, of course, is the wages of government employees—but even these are adjusted to compete with private market wages.

4. In market economies, unemployment rates tend to be well above zero percent because of the natural dynamics of movements into and out of the labor force and because of the decline of certain sectors that become victims of the process of creative destruction.

5. This does not imply that the East German economy was efficient. There were many mutually beneficial exchanges that did not occur because of the inefficient resource allocation.

6. This comparison should not diminish the transition experience of the Czech Republic, which is also performing extremely well.

7. Inflation has consistently come down since then. At the end of 1995 the inflation rate fell to under 2 percent once again, and it was only 1.9 percent in 1997.

8. *New York Times*, "Germany, Bundesbank Clash Over Currency Maneuver," May 29, 1997.

9. *New York Times*, "Europeans Clear Remaining Hurdle to Currency Unity," February 28, 1998. The deficit was reduced in part by raising the sales tax to 16 percent.

10. J. Barkley Rosser Jr. and Marina V. Rosser, *Comparative Economics in a Transforming World Economy* (Chicago: Irwin, 1996). The discrepancy between the one-in-three perception and the 16 percent recorded unemployment is due to the fact that many who lost their jobs dropped out of the labor force.

11. *New York Times,* "Analysis: Will Gamble on Eastern Germany Pay Off?" April 17, 1997.

12. This policy is risky. If the government allows domestic inflation to exceed significantly the rate of inflation in the economy to which the currency is tied, which leads to a sharp devaluation, then the credibility of the government and the effectiveness of the fixed exchange rate policy may be muted.

13. Exchange rate risk is the risk that the price of an internationally traded good or service will unexpectedly change in the time between the signing of the contract and the payment date because of an unanticipated change in the exchange rate. For example, suppose that US$1 is equal to 1 zloty. A Polish firm contracts to purchase $100 of wheat, expecting to pay 100 zloty. If there is a devaluation of the zloty such that $1 is now equal to 2 zloty, then the Polish firm will have to pay 200 zloty in order to service the $100 payment.

14. World Bank, *World Development Report,* 1996, p. 64.

15. Stanley Fischer, Ratna Sahay, and Carlos A. Vegh, "Stabilization and Growth in Transition Economies: The Early Experience," *Journal of Economic Perspectives,* vol. 10, no. 2 (Spring 1996), p. 58.

16. Josef C. Brada, "Privatization Is Transition—Or Is It?" *Journal of Economic Perspectives,* vol. 10, no. 2 (Spring 1996), pp. 67–86.

17. Brada, "Privatization Is Transition—Or Is It?" p. 76.

18. *World Development Report,* p. 108.

8

Poland and Russia in Transition

Poland was the first of the Central and Eastern European nations to begin the process of transition from socialism to capitalism. Transition began in 1989, and Lech Walesa, the leader of the Solidarity trade union responsible for much of the dissent against Communism, was elected president in a democratic election in 1990. Poland imposed shock therapy on its economy; market reforms and new policies were implemented quickly, with little planning or direction. Output plummeted at first, but rebounded quickly. Poland seems to have turned the corner to successful transition. The Soviet Union was dissolved at the end of 1991, and Russia formally became an independent republic. Russia also imposed shock therapy on the economy, but its economic performance has been disastrous. In this chapter we discuss the transitions of Poland and Russia and explore the reasons for the divergent performance of these two economies.

Poland

Germany invaded Poland on September 1, 1939, and started World War II in Europe. During the war Stalin created the Polish Workers' Party, which took power after Germany's defeat in 1945. By 1947 Poland's democratic system had been dismantled and Soviet-style Communism was firmly in place. Stalin imposed five-year plans, state ownership of assets, and heavy industrialization. Despite the Soviet influence, Poland had never been considered a "hard-core" socialist economy. It allowed more political and economic freedom than other Soviet-controlled nations, and there was more resistance to Communist control. For example, Polish agriculture was never collectivized, although there was a significant state farm sector; private farms survived to the end. There were also frequent strikes and riots in opposition to rising food prices.

Macroeconomic performance in Poland was typical of socialist nations. In the 1950s and 1960s, growth rates were fairly high as the economy exploited natural resources and increased its industrial base. But beginning in 1970, growth rates plummeted, bottoming out in 1980. The government responded by scaling back state planning, and it gave firms more managerial and price-setting control. Poland's debt increased significantly in the 1980s, however, and inflation increased to over 250 percent in 1989. The economic chaos led to new strikes, a new non-Communist government, and, finally, democratic elections whose victors launched the transformation to capitalism.

The task of transforming the institutional framework of the Polish economy began in earnest. The first major reform, known as the Balcerowicz Plan, was implemented in January 1990.[1] This plan abolished remaining price controls, lifted foreign exchange restrictions, devalued the Polish zloty and pegged it to the U.S. dollar, legalized ownership of private assets and enterprises, reduced subsidies to SOEs, and taxed firms whose wages increased more than 30 percent above the rate of inflation. This was done to stop the wage-price inflation spiral.

Table 8.1 lists the major economic indicators for Poland from 1989 to 1997. Poland's level of output fell sharply in 1990 and 1991, but rebounded quickly. Growth has been positive and strong in every year since 1993. Unemployment has been more of a concern. Under socialism the government provided universal employment, so unemployment rates were extremely low. With the transition to capitalism unemployment increased each year to its peak level of 16 percent in 1994, though it has fallen dramatically since then, to 10.8 percent in January 1998. Part of the long-term success of Poland's economy will lie in its ability to fully employ its citizens, an objective that Poland seems well on its way to accomplishing.[2]

Macroeconomic Issues

As described in the previous chapter, there were five major macroeconomic issues that Poland had to address. These were controlling inflation, reducing the deficit, stabilizing the currency, opening the economy to foreign trade, and attracting foreign investment. Poland has made good to excellent progress in all these areas in a very short period.

Poland managed to bring its inflation rate down quickly, from over 500 percent in 1990 to just 35 percent in 1993. The initial burst of inflation was due to price liberalization and monetary overhang combined with a shortage of goods and services. Devaluation of the zloty also increased the prices of Polish imports, which fueled inflation. But once the initial devaluation was complete and relative prices stabilized, inflation began to fall. By 1992 the inflation rate was under 50 percent the limit below which many economists believe the rate must remain for economic

TABLE 8.1   Key Statistics for Poland

Year	Growth Rate[a]	Inflation Rate	Unemployment Rate	Budget Deficit[b]	Exports[c]	Exchange Rate[d]
1989	0.5	251.1	0.3	7.3	7,575	N/A
1990	–11.6	586.0	6.1	–3.2	10,863	9,500
1991	–7.0	70.3	12.0	6.5	12,760	10,576
1992	2.6	43.0	14.0	6.7	13,997	13,626
1993	3.8	35.3	15.7	2.9	13,600	18,115
1994	5.5	32.2	16.0	2.3	16,000	22,723
1995	7.0	27.8	14.9	2.0	22,000	24,250
1996	6.0	18.5	13.6	2.5	24,350	26,961
1997	5.6	13.0	12.6	N/A	26,279[e]	32,793

[a] Percent change in real GDP.
[b] Percent of GDP.
[c] Millions of U.S. dollars.
[d] Zloty per U.S. dollars. On January 1, 1995, Poland redenominated the zloty at 10,000 to 1. These exchange rates do not reflect this redenominated value.
[e] Estimate.
SOURCES: Growth and inflation rates: 1989–1995 from *World Development Report*, 1996, pp. 173–174; 1996 from *Transition Newsletter*, vol. 8(1), February 1997; 1997 from OECD, www.oecd.org. Unemployment rates: 1989–1992 from Rosser and Rosser, *Comparative Economics in a Transforming World Economy*, p. 299; 1993–1994 from Schnitzer, *Comparative Economic Systems*, p. 281; 1995–1996 from Polish embassy, www.poland-embassy.org.uk /economy/econ12.htm; 1997 from OECD, www.oecd.org. Budget deficit: 1989–1993 from *Poland: The Path to a Market Economy*; 1994–1995 from *International Financial Statistics*, April 1997; 1996 from U.S. and Foreign Commercial Service, *Country Commercial Guide: Poland*. Exports: 1989–1993 from *Poland: The Path to a Market Economy*, p. 103; 1994–1997 from *International Financial Statistics*, April 1998. Exchange rates: *International Financial Statistics*, April 1998.

growth to occur. It has remained under 50 percent since then, and inflation for 1997 was only 13 percent.

Poland has been able to control its budget deficit mainly because it has been able to limit its government expenditures. In fact expenditures as a percentage of GDP were nearly identical in 1988 (the last year before transition) and 1993. In 1989 the deficit-to-GDP ratio peaked at nearly 8 percent, but it has fallen since then.[3] In 1990 the government ran a surplus as a result of a sharp one-time cut in government expenditures.

Poland's tax system has been completely revamped. Four major taxes were imposed. The enterprise income tax (EIT), implemented in 1989, taxes business income at a rate of 40 percent. A 2 percent tax is levied on the gross payroll of enterprises to finance unemployment insurance. A personal income tax is assessed, with the highest tax rate at 40 percent. Finally, a value-added tax (VAT) was introduced, with the highest rate at 22 percent.[4] To encourage tax compliance and reduce tax arrears, penalties were increased that included stiff fines and imprisonment. Moreover, the number of employees in the tax offices went from 23,600 in mid-1990 to 32,390 at the end of 1993. More than 6,000 people were employed in the new fiscal police force.[5]

The Polish zloty was initially devalued on January 1, 1990, and set at a rate of 9,500 zloty per U.S. dollar. The Poles adopted a fixed exchange rate tied to the dollar to serve as an anchor for inflation expectations. Inflation far exceeded price increases in the United States, forcing Poland to devalue its currency. In May 1991 the zloty was no longer pegged to the dollar but to a "basket" of currencies, including the U.S. dollar and European currencies. On October 15, 1991, the zloty was switched to a preannounced crawling peg. This allowed Poland to have a higher inflation rate than in the countries to whose currency the zloty was tied, and to remain competitive internationally. Between 1989 and 1996, Polish exports more than tripled.

Poland has also made progress toward liberalizing its trade institutions and promoting foreign investment. In January 1990 a new customs law went into effect that harmonized tariff rates along broad product classifications. In 1992 Poland lowered or eliminated tariffs on many products traded with the European Union (EU) in an effort to gain admittance to the union. Though trade laws are somewhat erratic, much progress has been made since the transition. Foreign investment is governed by the Foreign Investment Act of 1991. The act was intended to establish equal rules between foreign and domestic investors. Any level of foreign ownership, up to 100 percent, is allowable. Poland's attempt to attract foreign investment has been somewhat successful. The ratio of foreign direct investment to 1994 GDP was 0.70. Relative to the twenty-eight other transition economies, Poland had the fourth highest rate of investment, behind Hungary, Albania, and the Czech Republic.[6] Poland has not embraced foreigners as quickly and excitedly as Hungary has, but neither has it shut them out. In fact Poland recently amended its trademark law, and it imposed a new copyright law in June 1994. These institutional changes make it safer and more desirable for foreign businesses to invest in the Polish economy, because they better protect intellectual property rights. It is more difficult for someone in Poland to copy and resell the technology of a foreign producer. On the whole, Poland's macroeconomic performance has been quite good. It has managed to contain inflation, it has sustainable budget and trade deficits, the currency valuation is predictable, and trade is growing quickly.

Microeconomic Issues

On the microeconomic front are the issues of price liberalization, privatization, formation of capital markets, and development of a legal market framework. Poland quickly chose to free most prices from central control. The response was a surge in prices for many goods and services, but a reduction in resource inefficiencies, and incentives for suppliers to enter new markets and increase production.

Privatization has been a mixed bag in Poland. The institutional framework was changed in 1990 to legalize all forms of private enterprise. At the end of 1994, 55 percent of Poland's GDP was produced in the private sector.[7] This was a higher percentage than all other transition economies except the Czech Republic. Transfer to private ownership has been quick and easy in many service and retail sectors, and the number of business startups has been considerable. The agricultural sector is largely privatized, but this was true before 1989 as well. The main difficulty in privatization has been with the large industrial SOEs. The Polish government has been reluctant to privatize these giant firms, for economic and political reasons. Of the 7,841 SOEs in Poland, only 1,308 of them (16.7 percent) had been privatized by the end of 1994.[8] The slow pace of privatization is a result of a fear of unemployment and a fear of foreign ownership of large industries.

There are signs that Poland is becoming more serious about privatization. Poland's new privatization plan, adopted in 1996, called for the selling of about 120 large and medium-sized companies in 1997, together with about 300 smaller firms, with most state-owned assets being privatized by the year 2000. Two recent events attest to the government's desire to privatize. First, Poland recently put its petroleum industry up for sale. This sector is typically one of the most sensitive for a government to sell because of the sure source of revenue. Second, Gdansk Shipyard, the historic shipyard where the Solidarity movement began in the early 1980s, is on the auction block. Ironically, the shipyard filed for bankruptcy in 1996 with debts of $120 million, a victim of market competition. Greek, Canadian, and Belgian entities are bidding for the assets.[9]

Capital market reform has proceeded more smoothly. The banking system had to be completely overhauled. Before the transition the National Bank of Poland (NBP) had a monopoly on central bank functions and commercial banking activity. In 1989 the NBP was broken up into nine state-owned commercial banks, two of which have been privatized. In addition, more than ninety private banks have formed, and they serve a significant share of the banking market. The NBP now focuses on its role as a relatively independent central bank, regulating the money supply mainly by pegging the exchange rate. The NBP is required each year to submit a draft of its monetary policy guidelines to parliament. The Warsaw Stock Exchange, which had closed in 1939, was reopened in July 1991. Strict institutions define the rules for listing and trading stocks on the exchange. Regulation and enforcement is carried out by a newly created organization called the Securities Commission. The Stock Exchange is still very thin—that is, only a small number of companies are listed—but volume has grown considerably. The Polish bond market is very limited because of the lack of investment banks, whose expertise is required to help firms through the complex debt issue process. Most firms in Poland finance investment from corporate profits. However, the institutional framework is in place for capital markets to mature and grow.

Finally, demonopolization policy is beginning to take root in Poland. An antimonopoly law was put into effect on July 4, 1995, giving the Antimonopoly office a broad range of powers.[10] The office has the authority to investigate monopoly behavior toward consumers, and it must approve applications for mergers. With time, this organization will become more effective.

Political and Social Issues

Political democratic institutions have progressed quite rapidly in Poland. As mentioned earlier, Poland has always been one of the more democratic socialist nations. It should not be surprising, then, that transition first took root there. Since the transition, there have already been two peaceful, uncorrupted elections, and the National Assembly adopted a new constitution on April 2, 1997. Freedom House constructed a Democratic Rights Index, which was aggregated and reported by Peter Murrell to measure the degree of democracy in various transition countries. In 1989 Poland received a score of 58; by 1994 the score had increased to 83. By comparison, the mean value of all transition economies was 25 in 1989, and 56 in 1994.[11]

Poland has also done quite well in developing a social safety net. In pre-transition Poland, the safety net was based on participation in the labor market and the subsidization of key consumer goods. All employed people had access to old-age pensions, disability compensation, health care, workers' compensation, sick pay, family allowances, and maternity benefits.[12] Many benefits were provided directly by the employee's SOE. This system had the advantage of being comprehensive, but it disguised many of the underlying social problems such as worker dissatisfaction. In today's free-market economy, in which workers can be hired and fired and prices are set in the market, an employment-based, consumer-subsidized safety net no longer makes sense. The posttransition safety net had to be reformulated. The Employment Law established unemployment benefits in December 1989. The benefits were initially very generous and carried no time limit, though they have since been scaled back. Consumer subsidies were eliminated. Poland has continued its pension system with minor reforms, and sick benefits and health care are still provided. Despite these social programs, poverty increased during the transition, because of the large drop in output and the rapid rise in unemployment. Moreover, income distribution widened, leaving those on the lower end of the distribution with less income. Massive poverty and starvation did not occur, however. Average daily calorie intake between 1989 and 1992 declined just 5 percent, and meat and fish consumption increased. Perhaps more telling is that the infant mortality rate declined during the transition. Poland managed to reinvent its social safety net in a relatively short time. While poverty rates did increase, a social crisis was avoided.

The experience of Poland suggests that shock therapy is a possible alternative for transition economies when more gradualist approaches may not be politically feasible. Poland quickly tore down its socialist fabric and replaced it with formal institutions necessary for the operation of a market economy. Macroeconomic performance has been strong for the past six years. Poland had two initial conditions that strongly aided the transition process. First, there was some semblance of capitalist market institutions during the period of socialist rule. Private markets existed, though they were not promoted by the state. The Poles also had more freedom than citizens of other socialist nations and had more exposure to Western ideas, products, and culture. Many knew how a market economy could function, and eager Poles took advantage of the new economic freedom to establish small businesses. Second, there was almost a national consensus for transformation to capitalism, or at least to something besides socialism. Little time or energy was wasted in deciding whether or not to make the transition. There were no widespread efforts to turn back the change and return to socialism. This does not imply, however, that everyone is content with the reforms. The hardships in the transition have brought about a political backlash. In fact, Lech Walesa, the leader of the Solidarity trade union responsible for instigating much of the transition process, was voted out of office in 1995 after serving just one term. A left-wing party candidate, Aleksander Kwasniewski, is now the president of Poland. Nevertheless, Poland seems to be on the path to a successful transition to a capitalist economy.

Russia

The Russian transition has been very different and more problematic than Poland's. Russia is the largest of the former Soviet republics, with 51.4 percent of the population, and 76 percent of the land area. It has a population just short of 150 million, and its land area is nearly twice the size of the United States. Russia is rich in natural resources; it is the world's largest producer of natural gas, third in petroleum production, and fourth in the mining of coal.[13] Despite its resources, Russia's post-transition economic performance has been very poor. Russia has not been able to stop the downward spiral and begin the process of economic reconstruction. Its political, economic, and social institutions are in disarray, and the health problems of President Yeltsin have left the country with weak and inconsistent leadership. Unlike Poland, Russia had no history of a market-based institutional framework to rely on when the transition began; the Soviet Union had destroyed its private economy more thoroughly than had other socialist nations. Nor was there a clear mandate for radical reform in Russia. The battle between Yeltsin and Mikhail Gorbachev for control of Russia in the late 1980s and early 1990s left the average Russian torn and confused. Gorbachev was becoming increasingly irrelevant, and Yeltsin seemed to be a loose cannon without a coherent plan for change. Although there have not been any successful attempts to turn back the tide of transition in Russia, one senses that the possibility is still present. This section provides first a brief history of pre-Communist Russia and the Soviet Union and then a detailed description of the recent transition process.

From 1547 to 1917, Russia was a feudal agricultural economy ruled by a hereditary line of czars. Czars granted land to the gentry, who then gave the czar financial support. Peasants were required to work the land and serve in the military. Though serfdom was abolished in 1861, most peasants had no land and had to work as farm hands. In the late nineteenth century, Russia began to industrialize as a result of an increase in foreign capital. All the capital was concentrated in Moscow and St. Petersburg, however, leaving most of Russia's economy based on agriculture. Even in 1913, 51 percent of Russia's output was from agriculture, and 28 percent came from industry.[14] Some think that capitalism was beginning to take root in the early 1900s and that the Bolshevik Revolution interrupted the process. Nevertheless, any seedlings of capitalism before the Communist takeover were small and weak.

Internal chaos brought about by economic disorder and ethnic conflict led to a revolution in March 1917. Food shortages led to riots and the eventual abdication of the last czar, Nicholas II. In October of that year the Bolsheviks, led by Lenin, took power from an interim government. Lenin declared all land to be property of the state, and industrial enterprises were run by committees. More complete Communism came to the Soviet Union under Stalin in the late 1920s. Stalin wished to industrialize the nation quickly. To do so, he collectivized agriculture and established production targets for each sector in his five-year plans. The steel industry was given top priority, and other sectors, especially agriculture, suffered from lack of resources. Political freedom was completely eliminated. Stalin caused the death of perhaps 20 million people during the 1930s, and he ordered the execution of anyone who seemed to pose a threat to his rule.

A succession of Soviet leaders ruled during the Cold War years. In 1985 Mikhail Gorbachev took control as general secretary and president of the Soviet Union. He set in motion political and economic reforms that unintentionally led to the collapse of Communism and the disintegration of the Soviet Union. Gorbachev initiated the policies of *perestroika* (restructuring) and *glasnost* (openness). His reforms were aimed at increasing manufacturing productivity. He called for more worker discipline, gave blue-collar workers a 20 percent increase in wages, and increased state funding for investment. But these reforms either failed or had only modest success. In 1987 Gorbachev announced new reforms that abolished output targets and gave enterprises much more freedom to make decisions concerning wages, investment, and profit. He also allowed firms to negotiate directly with suppliers and customers. Eventually, enterprises were given some flexibility in setting prices, and farms were permitted for the first time to engage in private buying and selling.

Though these reforms were radical in the Soviet Union, they did almost nothing to promote competition. Output and productivity remained stagnant in the late 1980s and then collapsed in the early 1990s. Deficits and inflation increased. Moreover, the break of Poland, Hungary, Czechoslovakia, and East Germany from the grip of the Soviet Union created grumbling among the Soviet Republics for their own freedom. Soviet Republics began breaking away. In August 1991 an attempt to overthrow Gorbachev failed, and the entire Communist party was discredited. Russia, Ukraine, and the remaining republics declared their independence. On December 25, 1991, Gorbachev abdicated the presidency, and the Soviet Union ceased to exist.

Boris Yeltsin was the president of Russia, and he had the daunting challenge of leading the independent republic down the road to capitalism. Yeltsin selected Yegor Gaidar as his minister of finance in November 1991. Gaidar advocated a shock therapy plan similar to that carried out in Poland. On January 2, 1992, the plan was implemented. The prices of all but fifteen basic commodities such as bread and gasoline were decontrolled. Prices rose 200 to 300 percent. State subsidies and military spending were slashed in an attempt to reduce the budget deficit to 3 percent of GNP. A privatization plan was instituted, and the ruble was made partially convertible. The idea behind the plan was to sharply curtail the influence of the state in production and leave the free market to pick up the slack.

Russia's transition thus far has been difficult at best and a disaster at worst. Table 8.2 lists key economic statistics for the Russian economy

TABLE 8.2   Key Statistics for Russia

Year	Growth Rates[a]	Inflation Rate	Budget Deficit[b]	Exports[c]	Exchange Rate[d]
1990	−3.6	5.6	N/A	71.1	1.7
1991	−5.0	92.7	N/A	50.9	1.7
1992	−14.5	1,353.0	−6.6	42.4	415
1993	−8.7	896.0	−9.8	43.0	1,247
1994	−12.6	303.0	−10.7	67.6	3,550
1995	−4.0	190.0	−3.5	81.1	4,640
1996	−6.0	21.8	−3.3	89.1	5,560
1997	0.4[e]	11[e]	−3.5[e]	87.4	5,960

[a] Percent change in real GDP.
[b] Percent of GDP.
[c] Billions of U.S. dollars.
[d] Rubles per U.S. dollar, year end.
[e] Estimate.

SOURCES: Growth rates: 1900–1995 from *World Development Report*, 1996, p. 173; 1996 from *Transition Newsletter*, vol. 7(11–12), Nov.–Dec. 1996; 1997 from "Commercial Overview of Russia: Economic Profile," *BISNIS*, January 1998. Inflation rates: 1990–1995 from *World Development Report*, 1996, p. 174; 1996–1997 from "Commercial Overview of Russia: Economic Profile," *BISNIS*, January 1998. Budget deficits: 1992–1994 from Stanisislav Menshikov, "Russia's Economic Policy: Suggestions for an Alternative," *Transitions Newsletter*, vol. 8(2), April 1997; 1995 from *Transitions Newsletter*, vol. 7(1-2), Jan.-Feb. 1996; 1996–1997 from "Commercial Overview of Russia: Economic Profile," *BISNIS*, January 1998. Exports: 1990–1993 from Schnitzer, *Comparative Economic Systems*, p. 254; 1994–1997 from *International Financial Statistics*, April 1998. Exchange rates: 1990–1991 from Paul R. Gregory and Robert C. Stuart, *Comparative Economic Systems*. Boston: Houghton Mifflin Co., 1999. 1992–1997 from *International Financial Statistics*, April 1998.

from 1990 to 1997. Each year it seems that economists and politicians project that the next year is the year that Russia's economy will bottom out and turn around. It has yet to happen. GDP decreased 6 percent in 1996, succeeding even larger declines between 1991 and 1994. The informal economy has increased significantly (an issue to which we shall return), but the decline in the measured economy has more than offset that growth. Despite fiscal austerity, inflation rates exceeded 100 percent on an annual basis through 1995. It wasn't until 1996 that Russia's inflation rate fell under the 50 percent threshold that is seen as necessary to achieve economic growth. Budget deficits have been significantly lowered in 1995 and 1996. The ruble continues to devalue, though its rate of devaluation has become predictable. Finally, the export sector has performed dismally, dropping substantially through 1992 and then recovering between 1994 and 1996. This is in contrast to Poland, which tripled its exports between 1989 and 1996. Unemployment has been difficult to gauge in Russia. Officially, unemployment rates have been between 2 and 3 percent of the labor force. However, these figures only count those who claim unemployment insurance or job training. Credible estimates of Russian unemployment in 1996 range from 9 to 20 percent.

Macroeconomic Issues

As with Poland and the other transition economies, Russia has key macroeconomic and microeconomic issues to address. We begin with the macroeconomic concerns. Macroeconomic policy must provide a stable environment with low transaction costs that allow for investment and growth. This means controlling inflation, reducing the budget deficit, stabilizing the currency, opening the economy to foreign trade, and attracting foreign investment.

Russia has had trouble controlling inflation. Inflation rates have been high and erratic. The initial price liberalization touched off the hyperinflation of 1992, but rapid increases in the money supply sustained the inflation into 1993. In the Soviet Union the price system not only rationed consumer goods to the public but also generated profits for industrial enterprises, which then turned over those surpluses to the government. Government revenue collapsed along with the price structure, and the government resorted to printing money to pay its bills. The high inflation fed on itself. Many consumers had stored rubles as savings and for lack of available consumer goods. This monetary overhang quickly disappeared as inflation increased, because holders of rubles rightly concluded that the inflation would erode their savings. The result was more spending and more inflation. Moreover, the devaluation of the ruble in 1993 to one-third of its 1992 value led to an increase in import prices and further increased inflation. Inflation gradually declined from its peak in 1992 as the monetary overhang disappeared and the government reduced its deficit and subsidies. From 1994 to the present, inflation has been mainly the result of supply-side shocks with rapid price increases in previously subsidized goods such as electricity and fuel. In 1996 the Russian government finally got inflation rates under control, but only by severely curtailing government spending.

Public finance has probably been the single largest macroeconomic problem for Russia during the transition. As suggested earlier in Table 8.2, deficits have indeed been under control since 1995, at 3.5 percent of GDP. But these figures mask the harsh realities of the government's budget. Table 8.3 illustrates the components of that debt in more detail. Simply put, people are not paying their taxes.

The total amount owed to Russia's federal government in January 1997 exceeded US$12 billion, a large sum compared to projected 1997 govern-

TABLE 8.3   Public Financing in Russia, 1992–1996

	1992	1993	1994	1995	1996
Federal revenue	100	61.4	71	74.7	58.2
Federal expenditure	100	84.2	88.7	62.2	53.0
Revenue as percent of GDP	16.5	10.0	13.3	14.6	9.5

SOURCES: Stanislav Menshikov, "Russia's Economic Policy: Suggestions for an Alternative," *Transition Newsletter*, vol. 8(2), April 1997, and *New York Times*, "On the Road to Capitalism, Russia's Tax System Gets a Flat," February 19, 1997.

ment expenditures of about US$90 billion. The biggest culprits are large enterprises such as Avtovaz, Russia's largest car manufacturer, which has 111,000 employees. "According to estimates by the State Tax Service, 17 percent of corporate and other taxpayers comply fully and on time. Some 49 percent occasionally comply, and 34 percent simply flout the tax regime."[15] A famous maxim states that only death and taxes are certain. Apparently, in Russia, only death is certain. These firms blatantly ignore tax and pension laws, essentially daring the government to challenge them or shut them down. The government thus far has not acted, for fear of social unrest and because shutting down these firms would in most cases decrease revenue, at least in the short term. Yeltsin did recently threaten forced bankruptcy for firms that did not pay their back taxes, but most viewed this as a hollow threat. Personal income tax revenues are also extremely low, accounting for 7.5 percent of government revenues. This figure is about one-fourth the levels in Western Europe. In the United States individual income taxes account for 44 percent of federal revenue.

In the context of the government's inability to collect revenue, expenditures had to be sharply cut. It is surprising how low Russia's deficits are given the decline in revenues. Even with the spending cuts, the government is millions of dollars in arrears on pension payments and wages to government employees. The 1997 budget called for further cuts in the already drained military budget. Military spending was to be cut from US$18.2 billion to $14.5 billion.[16] Subsidies to SOEs have already been cut from 16 percent of government expenditures to less than 10 percent, but further cuts are necessary. These budget cuts are occurring in the context of an economy that is still reeling from the transition. Standard Keynesian macroeconomic theory suggests that reductions in government expenditures will, other things being equal, lead to further declines in output and income. In other words, the government should ideally be increasing its expenditures on goods and services. The problem is that this approach might reignite inflation, and the government spending may simply support inefficient firms.

The ruble has consistently fallen since the transition began. The exchange rate stood at 1.7 rubles to the U.S. dollar in 1991; in March 1998 the rate was nearly 6,100.[17] Inflation accounts for a significant portion of this devaluation. With the reduction of inflation to less than 50 percent, the ruble has started to stabilize. However, capital flight is also to blame. When capital leaves Russia, demand for foreign currency rises, further devaluing the ruble. Capital flight occurs when property rights to financial assets are not secure, when the financial structure in an economy is weak, when devaluation is imminent, or when organizations hide funds, often raised illegally. All of these sources of capital flight have been important in Russia. Estimates are that organized crime groups in Russia account for at least 40 percent of the capital flight. Profits earned internally or those earned from foreign trade are transferred outside of Russia into foreign banks, where they are much more difficult to track. The Russian government has announced exchange rate bands that it supports. If the value of the currency falls below the stated band, the government steps in to buy the ruble and raise its price. Over time, these bands have been revised to adjust for inflation.

Russia has taken only limited steps to open its economy to foreign trade. The web of complex and conflicting formal institutions makes it prohibitively expensive for many foreigners to import goods to Russia. Goods entering the country are potentially subject to three taxes: an import duty, a value-added tax, and an excise tax. Customs procedures are constantly revised and are far from transparent. This increases the payoff to corruption, as key officials can move the process along for a fee.

For several years during the transition importers could claim to purchase goods that were in fact fictitious and send payment abroad, which aided capital flight in Russia. An importer could claim, for example, to purchase US$100,000 worth of clothing, and convert rubles to dollars and then send them abroad for payment. In fact, what the importer was doing was investing dollars abroad instead of holding the less stable ruble. On January 1, 1996, the Central Bank of Russia instituted an import passport system, which requires that the importer's bank issue a "passport" for payment of a specific import contract. The importer has 180 days to document the entry of the goods (including the quantity and quality) with Russian Customs or return to Russia the currency issued in payment for the goods.[18]

Russia has experimented with *free economic zones* (FEZs) on a very limited basis. These are areas in which trade laws are greatly simplified via reduced paperwork and low or zero tariff rates. To date, only Kaliningrad is truly a FEZ, though twenty-five regions in all have declared themselves to be or have been declared FEZs. These other regions, however, are still mired in legislative and bureaucratic red tape that has stunted their ability to attract foreign investment.[19] Estimates are that foreign trade in 1997 was slightly less than that in 1996, largely because of energy price declines. Russia must reform its trade institutions if it wishes to become more competitive internationally. The maze of complex trade rules partially shields domestic competitors from foreign competition and inhibits the Schumpeterian process of creative destruction.

The last major macroeconomic issue is attracting foreign investment. Russia has not performed well on this count at all. Between 1991 and 1996, Russia received US$6 billion in foreign investment. Estimates of capital flight between 1991 and 1996, in contrast, range from $50 billion to $150 billion.[20] "According to some estimates, total foreign direct investment in Russia amounted to $47 per person, compared with more than $300 for neighboring Poland."[21] Russia has taken some steps to attract foreign investment. The USSR Law on Foreign Investment, which remains in effect today, permits 100 percent foreign ownership of businesses, and in 1994 President Yeltsin issued a decree to streamline the business registration process. Furthermore, there are few restrictions on repatriating profits earned in Russia.[22] Despite these reforms, foreign investors perceive that the transaction costs of doing business in Russia are too high. Insecure property rights, a complex and ill-functioning legal system, and the dangers of organized criminal activities have kept foreign funds out of the country.

Overall, the macroeconomic transition has been poor. Inflation has been high, growth rates have been negative, the currency has continually devalued, and foreign trade and investment have been low, especially compared to Poland, Hungary, and the Czech Republic. But there has been progress since 1996. Perhaps that year was a turning point for stability as inflation and budget deficits were brought under control. Early data for 1997 suggest that the GDP has stabilized. Macroeconomic stability has to accompany and complement microeconomic transformation. We now turn to microeconomic issues.

Microeconomic Issues

On the microeconomic side, the key issues are price liberalization, privatization, formation of capital markets, and the creation of a legal system to establish property rights, to enforce contracts, and to promote competition. The shock therapy program implemented in January 1992 liberalized most prices. Since then other key prices have gradually increased to approach their true market value. The result has been a decrease in the inefficient allocation of resources, but also a dramatic increase in poverty, as incomes have not kept pace with price rises.

Russia has made considerable progress in privatizing its assets. In fact, given the size of the operation, one could argue that the privatization program has been as successful as any among the transition economies. This does not imply, however, that privatization has gone smoothly. There have been many problems, particularly in agriculture.

The Yeltsin government formally announced a privatization program a few months after price liberalization. Assets had to be privatized in both the nonagricultural and the agricultural sectors. In the nonagricultural transition, efforts were devoted to privatizing the state sector instead of encouraging the creation of new firms.[23] Small enterprises were sold off to private groups, and larger enterprises were converted into joint-stock companies with shares sold to workers, managers, the public, and the state. A voucher system was used, under which each citizen received a voucher for 10,000 rubles (about US$20). The holders of the vouchers could sell their vouchers to other investors at market prices set by commodity exchanges, or they could swap them for shares of a joint-stock company. The system was set up in such a way as to give workers and managers dominant shares of ownership of their enterprises. The most popular way to accomplish this was a provision that allowed 51 percent of the shares to be sold to workers at 1.7 times the enterprise's January 1992 book value. Vouchers could be used to purchase up to one-half of the shares. The public could then bid for the remaining 49 percent.[24] By the end of 1995, 66 percent of medium-sized and large Russian enterprises were in private hands; 55 percent of total state assets were transferred by management-employee buyouts.[25]

In November 1995 a new phase of privatization was initiated. The government began auctioning off 136 enterprises considered to be the most lucrative. The industries privatized or put up for sale include utilities, long-distance telephone, power and gas enterprises, and railroads. In mid-1997, revenues from these industries exceeded projections.[26]

Privatization in agriculture has been much less successful. By 1993 only 38 percent of agricultural production was from private sources.[27] The reason is that the government has made it difficult and complex to privatize farms, and Russian farmers have been very hesitant to take the risks involved in private enterprise. Russia had very limited experience with private ownership of land even before Stalin collectivized farms. As a consequence, even when farmers were given the option of privatizing, most chose to remain in the collective communities. Some of the early risk takers were hazed and threatened by the more conservative farmers. Even Yeltsin has been hesitant in giving farmers easy access to private land. He did not issue far-reaching land decrees until October 1993, and even then he "continued to encumber the land privatization effort with all kinds of regulations, procedures, and committees, presumably to prevent corruption and to promote equity."[28] There was a ten-year ban on the sale of land used for communal farming. Only the small garden plots that many peasants and urban dwellers farmed could be sold. The regulations were meant to prevent land speculation, but they also dramatically slowed the process of agricultural privatization. In March 1996 Yeltsin issued a decree that owners of farmland could buy, sell, or mortgage their land provided that it stays in agricultural use. However, the legislature has been trying to overturn this law. Therefore, property rights to land remain confused and unstable.

The third microeconomic issue is to transform and develop capital markets to facilitate the process of saving and investing. This has been a difficult task. Banking reform began in 1988 before the breakup of the Soviet Union. The Russian Gosbank was broken up into two components: a central bank (now called the Central Bank of the Russian Federation) and a group of commercial banks. In 1990 a banking law allowed the establishment of joint-stock banks. Moreover, some of the large state banks were broken up into independent regional banks. In 1989 there were five banks in Russia; by 1995 there were more than 2,500. The explosive growth in commercial banking has led to a mainly private but extremely fragile banking system. Many of the new commercial banks were set up with little capital and little regulation, and they made a profit by speculating on the currency markets. Banks could take rubles and convert them into dollars (or other foreign currencies), hold the dollars for a time, and then convert them back into more rubles after the ruble devalued. Checking accounts do not exist. Loans predominantly finance inventories and receivables, and are very short-term. Loans for investment are rare. Moreover, many of the loans made are interbank loans.

Transaction costs in the banking sector are very high. This is true both for deposits and loans. Deposits make up a very small percentage of bank assets in part because there is no deposit insurance in Russia. Only the state-controlled savings bank (Sberbank) guarantees deposits. Depositors in other banks have no way of knowing that their funds will be safe. A 1995 survey indicated that 53 percent of Russians preferred to keep their savings out of banks.[29] The high transaction costs also reduce the banks' ability to make loans. Measurement costs are extremely high, because financial information about a potential borrower is false, unreliable, or unavailable. Enforcement costs are also high. "Property rights are ill-defined, the legal status of collateral is unclear, and Russia still does not have laws governing such things as the order of claims in bankruptcies."[30] To reduce these transaction costs, banks must be monitored and supervised, some form of deposit insurance is required, a whole set of accounting institutions to report firms' financial condition must be created and enforced, and enforcement of lending contracts must be improved. Russia has begun to implement some of these reforms. In April 1995 the Central Bank of the Russian Federation was given authority to license new banks, supervise existing banks, and impose penalties or revoke banking licenses.[31] As of late 1997 there were roughly 1,700 banks in Russia, down from a high of 2,600 a few years earlier. The Central Bank had revoked a total of 715 commercial bank licenses by mid-1997.[32] Russia is also working on a project with the World Bank and the European Bank for Reconstruction and Development to introduce international banking standards to ensure proper management of commercial banks.[33]

Stock and bond markets also need to mature. The first Russian stock exchange was opened in the summer of 1991, and there are now more than 70 exchanges. Russia ranked fourth among transition economies at the end of 1995, with a market value of shares as a percent of GDP at 10 percent. Only the Czech Republic, the Slovak Republic, and China had larger percentages.[34] The problem is that these exchanges are unregulated. Pyramid schemes are common as false information and speculation drive up prices until the bubble bursts, leaving investors with worthless shares. As in the commercial banking sector, institutional changes are necessary that regulate access to the exchange and require accurate and consistent disclosure of financial information.

The last key microeconomic issue is to establish a legal framework that establishes property rights, enforces contracts, and promotes competition. Weak leadership has undermined property rights and enforcement systems in Russia. President Yeltsin has had severe heart problems and suffers from depression and suspected alcoholism. When he has not been in the hospital, his leadership has been erratic. He quickly dismisses key government officials (sometimes the entire Congress) whenever there is disagreement over the appropriate course of action, and he often reverses himself on strategy. In March 1998 he suddenly dismissed his entire cabinet. Consequently, there has never been a consistent legal framework. Yeltsin operates at times like a sovereign ruler issuing decrees at will. At times these decrees may be efficiency-enhancing, but at other times they are destabilizing. A more equal balance of power between the executive and the legislative branches would help to stabilize formal institutions.[35]

A more serious problem is with organized crime. Estimates are that the Russian Mafia controls more than 40 percent of the total economy. According to the Russian Interior Ministry, the number of registered crimes by organized groups has increased 94 percent since 1992. There are more than 9,000 such groups now operating in Russia, employing around 100,000 people. These groups have infiltrated the banking sector and the financial markets. They pay no taxes, and they force legitimate businesses to pay protection fees to continue operations. Most firms have no choice but to cooperate. "In 1994, the Yeltsin Government reported that seventy to eighty percent of private businesses were paying extortion money to organized criminal gangs. Eighty percent of all U.S. businesses in Russia have bribed a Russian government official at least once."[36] The Mafia also influences and bribes government officials directly. Under these circumstances, the government has lost the ability to adequately protect consumers and businesses. Recall from Chapter 4 that one of the most important roles of government is to act as an impartial arbiter in settling disputes. The Russian government has not fulfilled this role, because of its inability to control organized crime. The results are unstable property rights, high transaction costs, and dampened incentives for organizations to produce and advance technology.

Russia has also had a difficult time promoting competition. The Soviet Union prided itself in its massive industrialization. Often one or two firms supplied a given product to the entire country. Such a setup made planning easier and allowed the enterprises to take advantage of economies of scale. But this industrial organization made competition difficult to achieve during transition. The large SOEs had to be broken up into smaller units, but even after this process, a few large firms were left with considerable market power. Moreover, many of these firms have enough political and social influence to retain the state subsidies and shirk their tax obligations.

Enterprises operating under Communism in the Soviet Union were vertically linked so that one firm supplied the parts necessary for another firm to produce its output. For example, firm A produced steel and shipped its output to firm B. Firm B converted the steel into automobile frames and shipped the output to firm C. Firm C added tires, seats, and other components until the cars were completed. The result was a chain of bilateral monopolies. But like any chain, its strength was determined by the weakest link. If the steel production process shut down, the whole production process ground to a halt because firms further down the chain could not obtain steel from alternative suppliers. Though the privatization process brought competition to a few of the firms in the chain, other firms remained monopolies. The result has been a lack of competition throughout the production process. With little competition, firms have less of an incentive to engage in the process of creative destruction. The short-term solution is to continue to break up the large enterprises. The privatization of key state industries provides an opportunity to promote competition if the SOEs are broken up and sold to a number of private firms. The long-term solution is for new firms to enter the market to compete against existing firms.

Polish and Russian Transitions Contrasted

Poland is well on its way to good economic performance as a capitalist economy; Russia is not. Why is this so? There were many similarities in the Russian and the Polish transitions. Both used shock therapy to liberalize prices and to privatize assets rapidly. Over time the majority of subsidies to the SOEs were eliminated, and both countries have achieved macroeconomic stability. Democratic processes were implemented in both countries, and peaceful elections have been held. What accounts for the divergence of performance? The key lies in the differences in the institutional framework in the two countries. Poland has managed to create an environment in which the rules of the game are adequately spelled out, in which most people follow the rules so that uncertainty is manageable, and in which transaction costs are reasonably low. Russia has an economy plagued by crime, corruption, and high transaction costs. Recent research supports this view.

In a recent article, Timothy Frye and Andrei Shleifer proposed three models for governments in transition:[37] the *invisible-hand* model, the *helping-hand* model, and the *grabbing-hand* model. In the invisible hand model, the government is well organized and generally uncorrupt. It defines the institutional framework and allows market participants to allocate resources. The main role is to make sure everyone is playing by the rules. The helping-hand model is one in which governments are more actively involved in promoting private economic activity. The legal framework plays a limited role because the government is the direct arbiter of disputes. Corruption is present, but limited. The grabbing-hand model is one in which the government is again very interventionist, but less organized and much more corrupt. Government officials act in their own self-interest with few checks and balances. The government does not have the ability to enforce contracts or to ensure law and order.

Frye and Shleifer conducted a survey of fifty-five small shops in Moscow and fifty small shops in Warsaw. They focused on the legal and regulatory environment in each country. Survey respondents from both countries expressed considerable skepticism about the effectiveness of the legal environment, but two significant differences stood out. Participants were asked whether they needed to use the courts but did not do so. In Warsaw 10 percent of the respondents answered yes; 45 percent of Moscow respondents said yes. One interpretation of this is that shop owners in Moscow have relatively more legal disputes and less faith in the court system to settle those disputes. Respondents were also asked if they needed a "roof" in order to operate. A "roof" is a private security agency that protects firms from crime and helps to settle disputes. Only 6 percent of Polish business owners answered yes, whereas 76 percent of Russian owners reported that they need a roof in order to operate. This clearly indicates the high degree of crime in Moscow and the inability of the Russian government to enforce the formal institutions. The regulatory burden was also much greater in Moscow than in Warsaw. It took longer to register a business in Russia. There were twice as many inspections per year (eighteen as compared to nine in Poland), and bribes had to be paid to government officials more often. The authors concluded that although neither government fulfills the "ideal" role, the Polish government has been able to approximate the invisible-hand model of government. The Russian government more closely resembles the grabbing-hand model, which leads to high transaction costs and poor economic performance.

Because of the differences in the role of government between Poland and Russia, there has been a significant difference in the ability of organizations to respond to market incentives. Polish organizations have responded much more effectively to the profit motive, and production and incomes have increased. Poland has led the way in business startups in part because the regulatory environment is more friendly, allowing easier entry into the market. Polish entrepreneurs have at least an adequate level of faith in the existing system, and they are able and willing to participate. The process of creative destruction also has been stronger in Poland. The monopolistic structure in Russia hampered severely the response of organizations to the market system. As Marshall Goldman noted, "Shock therapy was predicated on the presence of supply flexibility within the system and mobility among the factors of production. But the existence of virtual monopolies in important industries made it unlikely that these industries would respond to market signals."[38] Moreover, the government continued to subsidize many of these firms in the early stages of transition, providing them with soft budget constraints. These monopolistic firms did not have to respond to competitive forces because there was no competition. Nor did they have to operate efficiently because the government was there to subsidize losses. The presence of the monopolies also limited the ability of start-up firms to compete against the former SOEs. The same problems with monopolies existed in Poland, but to a much lesser degree. Furthermore, capital markets in Poland functioned better than those in Russia, giving more organizations the financial backing necessary to enter the market. Russian capital markets have been fragile and plagued with high transaction costs, resulting in few loanable funds for investment.

One strong indication of the difficulty of organizational formation and the lack of enforcement of formal institutions in Russia is the growth of the informal economy. Informal economies are discussed in detail in the next chapter, but we can introduce the concept here. The *informal economy* is that gray area between completely legal economic activity and perfectly illegal economic activity.[39] The informal economy grows for two reasons. First, access to the formal economy is difficult. Second, firms decide to remain underground in order to avoid some of the costs of operating in the formal sector. In Russia, this second explanation seems more prevalent. But the informal sector can exist only if the government either chooses not to or is unable to stop its growth. In the formal economy businesses are heavily regulated and taxed by the government. To avoid such payments, many Russians choose to pay the local officials a fee for operating unofficially. The fee may be large, but it is less than the cost of operating in the formal sector. Thus informal economies imply that the grabbing-hand model of government is at work. The problem is that informal markets suffer from high transaction costs because the government does not fully recognize their existence, and therefore firms operating within informal markets are denied the right to court systems and other enforcement institutions. Moreover, property rights are insecure, subject to the whims of local bureaucrats. Therefore, firms in informal markets tend to remain small-scale and invest little. In Russia the percentage of 1994 GDP produced by the informal economy was estimated to be 40 percent. Before the transition the share of production by the unofficial economy was estimated at 10 to 15 percent of GDP. In contrast, Poland has a much smaller informal sector. The informal sector's share of 1994 GDP was estimated to be 15 percent, essentially unchanged from the Communist era.[40] In other words, Poland's formal institutions have encouraged the entry of organizations into the formal economy, but the formal institutions in Russia have led to the creation of a large informal sector with high levels of transaction costs and low levels of investment.

The roots of the differences in the posttransition economic performance of Poland and Russia probably lie in the culture and historical experiences of each country. Recall that before transition Russia was a poor agricultural economy with dictatorial rule and little experience with private ownership of resources. Stalin's rule of the Soviet Union only reinforced those trends. Poland, in contrast, had a history as a battleground for Russia, Germany, and Austria. Poland lost its nation status in 1795 when it was divided among Russia, Prussia, and Austria. Poland won its independence back in 1920 by defeating the Soviets. Though it had an authoritarian leader, private ownership of production prevailed, especially in agriculture. Communism never had a firm hold on Poles after World War II for several reasons. First, there was no history of Communism before the war. Second, Poles strongly resented Germany and Russia, both of which had invaded Poland during World War II and in the past. Third, the Catholic Church continued to have a strong hold in Poland despite the

imposition of Communism by Stalin. Finally, Poles have a history of re-
volting against their oppressors. Even at the height of the Cold War
Poland was more rebellious and more difficult to control than other Soviet
Republics. Hence it is not surprising that the collapse of the Soviet Union
began with the Polish move to establish a Western democratic society.

This difference in history and culture fundamentally affected attitudes
toward transition to capitalism and democracy. Poles were eager to cast
off Communism, and they had experience with private ownership of
production. Poles were willing to take the risks involved in establishing
private businesses. Indeed, Poland has outpaced its transition counterparts in new business formation. Though there was fear of change, people were optimistic about the future. A 1993 survey of attitudes toward
political and economic reform in Central and Eastern Europe showed
that people expected the future to be significantly better than the past.[41]
In such an environment of guarded optimism, most people would be
willing to follow the rules even if they did not necessarily like them. Russians, in contrast, were very fearful of change, as they had not had any
experience with private ownership or democratic rule. The same survey
showed that 80 percent of Russians had a favorable attitude toward the
past socialist economic system, and less than 40 percent had a favorable
attitude about the future. Moreover, "[p]olls in December 1991 suggested
that just over a quarter of Russians disagreed with the proposition that
ordinary people would benefit from the introduction of private property.
By March 1995 over two-thirds disagreed."[42] Unlike in Poland, the public attitude toward reform is deteriorating in Russia. In such an environment people perceive that the rules of the game are not fair. People will
try to cheat the system, since they do not believe in the changes. Others
who see the injustices that result from transition view change with deep
suspicion. The radius of trust is very short in Russia, which results in
high transaction costs, particularly when the government is incapable of
effectively enforcing transactions.

What is the solution for Russia? The Russian government must develop its formal institutions and enforcement mechanisms so as to bring
order to the chaos in the economy. Strong, fair, and effective leadership is
needed at all levels of government. Crime and corruption must be significantly reduced. The government must establish commercial codes and
enforcement mechanisms that work well. These things are easy to prescribe, but difficult to carry out. Informal institutions change very slowly;
a change in the formal rules may not result in changes in people's behavior. Russia is locked on a path-dependent track and significant reforms
will be very difficult to achieve. It has a long way to go, and there is no
reason to suspect that a true turnaround will occur in the near future.
Russia's economic and political future remains in doubt.

Questions for Discussion

1. Despite the superior performance of many capitalist economies over the past forty years, many citizens of Poland, Hungary, and Russia wish to go back to the "good old days" of socialist rule. Why do you think this is?
2. Why have Russia and the other former Soviet republics had a more difficult time than many Eastern European nations in making the transition from socialism?
3. The decision to transform to capitalism was easy for Poland but difficult for Russia. How do you think a nation's *attitude* about the willingness to become a capitalist nation affects its economic performance? Relate your answer to the theory of institutions developed in Chapters 4 and 5 of this book.
4. Is there a role for socialism in the economies of the next century? If so, what will that role be? If not, why not?

Notes

1. The plan was named after Finance Minister Leszek Balcerowicz.

2. This does not mean that unemployment must be reduced to zero, but to Poland's natural rate of unemployment. European unemployment rates have been high in the 1990s relative to the United States. Perhaps a respectable unemployment rate for Poland would be 8 or 9 percent.

3. Gerd Schwartz, "Public Finances," in *Poland: The Path to a Market Economy* (Washington, DC: International Monetary Fund, 1994).

4. A value-added tax is a tax on consumption, implemented to discourage consumption relative to saving and investment. Other things being equal, higher levels of investment result in higher levels of economic growth.

5. Schwartz, "Public Finances," p. 9.

6. Peter Murrell, "How Far Has the Transition Progressed?" *Journal of Economic Perspectives*, vol. 10, no. 2 (Spring 1996), p. 38.

7. Josef C. Brada, "Privatization Is Transition—Or Is It?" *Journal of Economic Perspectives*, vol. 10, no. 2 (Spring 1996), p. 77.

8. Ibid.

9. *Central Europe Online*, "Poland Could Sell Gdansk Shipyard," March 16, 1998.

10. Organization for Economic Cooperation and Development (OECD), *Annual Reports: Competition Policy in OECD Countries, 1994–95*, http://www.oecd.org/daf/ccp/ar-eng.htm.

11. Murrell, "How Far Has the Transition Progressed?" p. 28.

12. For an excellent summary of pre-transition and posttransition social institutions, see Gerd Schwartz, "Social Impact of the Transition," in *Poland: The Path to a Market Economy* (Washington, DC: International Monetary Fund, 1994), pp. 80–88.

13. U.S. Department of Commerce, International Trade Association, *Business Information Service for the Newly Independent States (BISNIS)*, "Commercial Overview of Russia: Economic Profile," http://www.iep.doc.gov/bisnis/country/rusfed.htm, January 1998; hereinafter the web site is referred to as *BISNIS*.

14. Martin C. Schnitzer, *Comparative Economic Systems*, 7th ed. (Cincinnati: South-Western College Publishing, 1997), p. 243.

15. *New York Times*, "On the Road to Capitalism, Russia's Tax System Gets a Flat," February 19, 1997.

16. *New York Times*, "Russian Leaders Urge Cuts in Military and State-Subsidized Industries," May 22, 1997. This sum is only a fraction of the $260 billion or so spent for defense in 1997 in the United States.

17. On January 1, 1998, Russia redenominated the ruble such that one new ruble equaled 1,000 old rubles. Thus the actual exchange rate in March 1998 was 6.1, not 6,100.

18. *BISNIS*, "Commercial Overview of Russia: Foreign Trade," January 1998.

19. Ibid.

20. Louise I. Shelley, "The Price Tag of Russia's Organized Crime," *Transition Newsletter*, vol. 8, no. 1 (February 1997).

21. *BISNIS*, "Commercial Overview of Russia: Foreign Investment," January 1998.

22. Ibid.

23. Marshall I. Goldman, *Lost Opportunity: Why Economic Reforms in Russia Have Not Worked* (New York: W. W. Norton, 1994), p. 132.

24. Ibid., p. 137.

25. World Bank, *World Development Report*, 1996, p. 53.

26. *BISNIS*, "Commercial Overview of Russia: Economic Profile," January 1998.

27. Schnitzer, *Comparative Economic Systems*, p. 226.

28. Goldman, *Lost Opportunity*, p. 126.

29. *New York Times*, "In New Economy, Russians Cannot Rely on Their Banks," September 12, 1995.

30. "Russian Banking," *Federal Reserve Bank of San Francisco (FRBSF) Weekly Letter*, no. 95-35, October 20, 1995.

31. Ibid.

32. *BISNIS*, "Commercial Overview of Russia: Banking and Finance," January, 1998.

33. World Bank, *World Development Report*, 1996, p. 100.

34. Ibid., p. 108.

35. This does not necessarily mean that the institutions would be more efficient, but organizations in society could be more assured that the rules of the game would not shift so quickly and arbitrarily.

36. Scott P. Boylan, "Organized Crime and Corruption in Russia: Implications for U.S. and International Law," *BISNIS*, January 1998.

37. Timothy Frye and Andrei Shleifer, "The Invisible Hand and the Grabbing Hand," *American Economic Review: Papers and Proceedings*, vol. 87, no. 2 (May 1997), pp. 354–364.

38. Goldman, *Lost Opportunity*, p. 101.

39. Although there is no single definition of an informal sector, this one ties in well with the New Institutional Economics.

40. Daniel Kaufmann, "Why Is Ukraine's Economy—and Russia's—Not Growing? *Transition Newsletter*, vol. 8, no. 2 (March/April 1997).

41. World Bank, *World Development Report*, 1996, p. 12.

42. Ibid., p. 12.

9

Institutions and Economic Development

This book has argued that institutions are the most important determinant of economic performance. In a static sense, institutions define the costs of transacting and the ability of organizations to capture the gains from specialization and division of labor. In a dynamic sense, institutions define the incentive structure under which organizations operate and determine whether or not organizations undertake activities that advance technology. The key to economic growth, then, is in finding the right institutional framework that will unlock a nation's wealth potential. The focus of this chapter is on institutions in the less developed countries (LDCs), the developing market economies. They are distinguished from transition economies because they are not undertaking radical changes in their formal institutional framework. Developing economies may need to change their economic policies and improve the efficiency of the existing institutions, but, unlike transition economies, they do not need to completely overhaul the institutional structure.[1]

As noted in Chapter 1, most nations in the world are poor. Many of these economies are capitalist, not socialist. Socialism provides poor incentives for long-run growth mainly because of the absence of competition; but then why don't all capitalist economies succeed? The answer is exactly the same as in socialist economies: The institutional framework does not provide low costs of transacting and does not force organizations to adhere to the process of creative destruction.

There are numerous examples of unstable institutional frameworks in LDCs. A recent series of events in Ecuador provides an excellent example. In July 1996 Ecuador elected Abdala Bucaram as president. With the exception of the obnoxious political campaigning, the elections were peaceful and relatively uneventful. Ecuador has been under democratic rule with a new constitution since 1979, and transfers of power have been smooth since then. But in February 1997, just six months into the president's four-year term, the Congress voted Bucaram out of office by claiming that he was "mentally incapacitated." Despite the conjecture that the vote was done more for political and economic rather than psychological reasons, the Congress's action was constitutional. But the Congress elected a successor to Bucaram, Fabian Alarcon, in an appointment that was not constitutional. According to the constitution, power should have passed to the vice president, Rosalia Arteaga. Meanwhile, the original president, Bucaram, refused to step down, and the vice president and Alarcon both declared themselves the "official" president. Thus for a time Ecuador had three presidents. The solution came almost as quickly as the crisis had. The military in Ecuador is seen as the last arbiter of power, and the president must have the military's nominal support in order to function. Within two days of the congressional vote to oust the president, the military made it clear that it would honor the legal congressional vote and refuse to support Bucaram. Bucaram then stepped down, leaving two presidential candidates. After negotiations, a solution was worked out in which the vice president would become the official president for a short time, until Congress could change the constitution and appoint Alarcon as president. Within days, Alarcon was Ecuador's new president, to serve until August 10, 1998.

There are two points to be made regarding this incident. First, political institutions in Ecuador are much more unstable than in more developed industrial countries. The possibility of having three presidents simultaneously in the United States is absurd, because the rules of succession are clear and have been followed for over 200 years without incident. Second, as much can be learned by what did *not* happen in Ecuador as by what did happen. After a few days of uncertainty and negotiations, Ecuador's constitutional process remained intact. The military did not take power, and the transfer of power was handled peacefully. This suggests that Ecuador has made progress in stabilizing its institutions in recent years. The outcome could have been much worse.

Institutions in many nations are far more unstable than they are in Ecuador. At the extremes of political, economic, and social chaos are countries such as Somalia, Rwanda, and Haiti. These countries at times have no formal institutional foundations, because various organizations battle for power; the result is often mass starvation and crisis. Transaction costs in these countries are prohibitively high.

This chapter deals with two topics concerning developing countries. First, we discuss the extensive informal sectors found in many LDCs. We learn that the presence of these informal sectors is an indirect indication of high transaction costs. Second, we contrast the post–World War II experiences of Latin American nations with those of many Asian nations.

We compare import substitution policies with export-led policies and draw some conclusions from these experiences.

The Informal Economy

As noted in the previous chapter, the informal economy is difficult to define, and it has been defined differently by different people. Some use the term to refer to all activities outside of the legal system. This includes the sale of illegal items, the unreported economy, and the unrecorded economy. In this book we separate the informal economy from the purely illegal economy, which we call the black market or the *underground economy*. For example, selling illegal drugs is part of the underground economy because the government has explicitly declared the activity illegal and devotes resources to preventing its occurrence; every aspect of the illicit drug trade is illegal, and those involved try to avoid detection by the government. The *formal* economy consists of those operations that are completely legal, operating in the institutional framework as determined by the government. The informal economy consists of all those activities that fall into the gray area between the formal economy and the underground economy. It is a range of activities in which some aspects are illegal and others are legal. The government does not have an explicit policy to stop these sectors, but neither are they fully protected under the legal system.

The most common type of informal activity in developing economies is street vending. Street vending consists of all the small-scale vendors whom the government does not completely recognize as legal. Many are informal because they do not report their sales to the government and hence do not pay sales tax. Most do not have formal licenses to operate their businesses. However, governments have not declared these street vendors to be completely illegal and therefore do not have consistent rules to evict them. Some street vendors are more informal than others. Some vendors have portable carts that they set up in different locations every day or perhaps every month. They do not have licenses, record their sales, or pay any direct taxes to the government. Other vendors are more established. They set up in fixed locations and pay a monthly rent to the government for the right to use the sidewalk space. They may or may not have licenses or permits, but they do not issue receipts, nor do they pay sales taxes.

Another example of the informal economy is the transportation market. Taxi drivers in Ecuador, for example, have licenses to operate their vehicles, but they do not use meters as required by the law. A price is negotiated before the customer gets into the taxi. This substantially reduces the fares. Of the dozens of taxi rides I took in Ecuador on a recent visit, only one driver attempted to use the meter, and he quickly acquiesced when I objected to the high fare he was trying to charge. Many buses also are operated informally. The drivers collect standard fares but do not report total sales to the government. They simply pay a fee to be able to operate the bus routes.

A third example is informal housing. As cities have grown as a result of migration from rural areas, demand for land and housing has increased. A common way to acquire urban land in LDCs is by invasion. Dozens of people jointly plan and then carry out an invasion in which they target a particular plot of land and then quickly settle the land, often at night, and build simple, temporary structures on it. Once the people and structures are in place, it is very difficult (though by no means impossible) to evict them. If the government does not issue a decree or allow the use of force to remove the settlers, then the invasion is successful and the settlement becomes part of the informal economy. The government does not completely recognize the settlers' property rights to the land, but neither does it view the settlement as illegal. Over time the government may grant the squatters partial or full rights to the land, and the land and housing become less and less informal, until they finally merge into the formal economy.

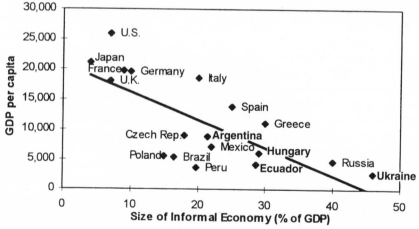

FIGURE 9.1   The Informal Economy and Per Capita GDP

NOTE: These percentages include the underground economy as well. The data for Latin America are not directly comparable, as they are based on employment data—urban informal underemployment as a percentage of total economically active population for 1980—rather than on output data.

SOURCES: *Transition Newsletter*, April 1997, *Economist*, Feb. 12, 1994, Eliana Cardoso and Ann Helwege, Latin America's Economy: Diversity, Trends, and Conflicts. Cambridge, MA: The MIT Press, 1992.

The informal sector is much larger in LDCs and former socialist economies than in the wealthier developed countries. Figure 9.1 plots the size of some informal economies (as a percentage of GDP) with GDP per capita. The negative relationship between a nation's standard of living and the size of the informal economy is demonstrated by the trend line in the chart. Why is this the case? As Hernando de Soto has explained, the informal economy grows when the legal system imposes rules that exceed the socially accepted legal framework and when the state does not have sufficient coercive authority to prevent operation of the informal economy.[2] In other words, compliance with the formal institutions is too costly and the government does not have the power to effectively enforce its costly rules.

Take street vending as an example. There are hundreds, sometimes thousands of street vendors in many cities in LDCs.[3] There is an obvious demand for their products—so why aren't these needs met by the formal economy? Part of the answer is that some choose vendors to remain informal in order to evade taxes and other regulations imposed on the formal economy. But, as explained later, these benefits to informality are small compared to the costs of informality. Those who choose to remain informal represent a small fraction of street vendors. The major obstacle to becoming formal is that the transaction costs of entering the formal economy are prohibitively high.

Recall that transaction costs are the costs of making, measuring, and enforcing agreements. Potential formal retailers must obtain permits from the government. Hernando de Soto estimated that it took 289 days to obtain permission to set up a small business in Lima, Peru. Moreover, two bribes had to be paid in order to obtain the license at all. To build a formal market, a place where a group of retailers could locate, took seventeen years.[4] Clearly the formal institutions inhibit the establishment of formal vendors and markets. The potential retailer must also be able to finance start-up costs until revenues are sufficient to cover expenses. The typical migrant to the city is very poor with little wealth, and so the only option may be to borrow the money from a bank or some other lender. The bank must be reasonably sure of being repaid, but with little collateral to offer, the potential retailer is a high risk. Therefore, the person may be forced into the informal sector, where start-up costs are much lower.

Ironically, the high transaction costs of becoming formal result in the creation of an informal economy plagued with inherently high transaction costs as well. As we saw in Chapter 4, for markets to work well the government must clearly specify and enforce property rights, and it must impartially enforce contracts. The government does none of these things in the informal sectors. In fact, it is the absence of these elements that defines, partially at least, what the informal economy is. Because the street vendor is not completely recognized by the government, his property rights to his location and to his assets are not fully secure. Moreover, the government does not recognize and therefore does not enforce the contracts of the street vendor. If the street vendor buys defective inventory from his suppliers, for example, he has no legal recourse to solve the problem. The result is a collection of street vendors who operate under conditions of high transaction costs.

With insecure property rights, the incentives for investment or expansion are severely diminished, because the risk of confiscation of assets is always present. Moreover, obtaining financing is much more difficult. It is also more difficult to transfer the business to another owner. Potential buyers must be sure that they have legitimate property rights to the assets of the business. These complications limit the size of the firm and result in numerous inefficient small firms that cannot take advantage of the economies of scale in retailing.

Absence of contract enforcement also results in high transaction costs. Vendors engage only in exchanges of small value for fear of being cheated. Moreover, almost all contracts are oral and paid for with cash, since credit is too risky. In efforts to enforce contracts, vendors may deal only with friends or relatives in repeat dealings, or they may resort to violence to "settle" a dispute. In this sense the informal economy is similar to the illicit drug trade in the black market. If a drug deal goes bad, the only way to enforce the contract or punish the cheater is by violence, since the government does not enforce illicit drug transactions. The drug dealer cannot turn to the police to complain that someone underpaid him for a drug shipment, so enforcement has to be internalized. The street vendor may have to use the threat of violence in order to increase contract compliance.

Similar results are found in the informal housing sector. When property rights to the land are insecure, occupants are reluctant to invest in the housing stock on the land. Hernando de Soto estimated that the formal housing stock in Lima was worth, on average, nine times that of the informal housing stock.[5] The informal economy is inherently plagued with high transaction costs, and hence those sectors are small-scale, unstable, and inefficient.

What is the solution? Hernando de Soto makes a convincing case that the answer is to absorb the informal economy into the formal economy. This prescription runs counter to the more common response by governments, which is to eliminate the informal economy or to reduce its size by enforcement of the formal institutions. If institutions were changed to significantly lower the costs of becoming formal, then many of the informal vendors could successfully make the transition. The new formal businesses could grow and hire as employees those who did not successfully transfer to the formal sector. Likewise, if governments offered relatively cheap access to secure land, migrants to the cities could construct decent shelters as their incomes increased. Many of the slum areas could be improved or even eliminated. The solution requires a change in institutions to lower the transaction costs of becoming formal.

Import Substitution Industrialization Versus Export-Led Policies

Recent history has given us another natural experiment in which we can assess the impact of two opposite development strategies. The preceding analysis of the informal sector dealt with the static model of institutions. Given the level of technology, an economy could increase its productivity and efficiency if it changed the institutions that blocked entry into the formal sector. In contrast, the analysis here focuses on the dynamic model developed in Chapter 5. In this section we look at the macroeconomic experiences of Latin America as contrasted with those of Asia. This regional comparative analysis has major exceptions, as India and China, for example, followed inward-looking policies. But the "typical" development policy in Latin America was inward looking, whereas that of East Asia was outward looking.

From approximately the 1930s through the early 1980s, Latin America pursued a policy of *import substitution industrialization* (ISI). As noted in Chapter 2, ISI is a policy initiative that advocates the adoption of institutions that encourage the development of domestic industry at the expense of industrial imports. The goal in Latin America was to replace the imported industrial goods with domestically produced industrial goods and thus to lessen their reliance on the developed economies for key products. Implementation of ISI included high tariffs and strict quotas on imports (especially finished manufactured items), diversion of resources from the export sector to finance the construction and expansion of domestic industry, direct government construction and operation of industries, and monetary intervention to overvalue the domestic currency.

In contrast to Latin America, many East Asian nations over the recent decades—notably Japan, Taiwan, Hong Kong, South Korea, and Singapore—have adopted *export-led policies*. The goal of these policies is to develop export sectors that are competitive in world markets. The engine of growth comes from expansion of exports. Implementation of export-led policies includes diversion of resources to producers of exports via lower tax rates and government subsidies of inputs, industrial policy to promote certain export-oriented sectors, and undervalued currencies that make exports more price competitive in world markets. The economic performance of the two regions pursuing very different policies can be compared, and some lessons can be drawn concerning institutions and economic growth.

Import substitution policies began almost by default in Latin America.[6] Because of the world depression, demand for exports was weak in the 1930s. Previously imported products either were not available or there was no foreign exchange to purchase them, because Latin America's terms of trade had fallen sharply. Therefore, Latin American countries looked inward to find the demand for traditional exports and to produce products that were previously imported. In this decade of depression, Latin American macroeconomic performance was better than the world average. It seemed that focus on internal demand had been a causal factor in economic growth.

During the late 1930s some Latin American economies began to reorient themselves to export production. However, World War II interrupted that transition. Again external demand was weak, and again Latin America was forced to look inward. Theoretical justification for ISI policies came from the Economic Commission for Latin America in 1948. Recall from Chapter 2 that the essence of the ECLA version of dependency theory was that the core trapped the periphery into a cycle of relative, if not absolute, poverty. Gains from trade were divided unequally at best, and the terms of trade for primary-goods producers deteriorated over time. The solution was to reduce the dependency of Latin America on imported manufacturing goods by producing these goods internally. By the end of the 1940s ISI policies were entrenched in Latin America.

Strong protectionist barriers were implemented, and foreign exchange from export earnings was funneled into industrial expansion. Currencies were overvalued to subsidize the importation of urban consumption goods and necessary capital equipment in the construction of new industries. An overvalued currency meant that the Mexican peso, for example, could purchase more foreign currency. Given an exchange rate of 5 pesos to the U.S. dollar, a $100 machine could be purchased for 500 pesos. But a stronger Mexican currency, with an exchange rate of, say, 3 pesos to the dollar, required only 300 pesos to purchase the same machine. The flip side was that Latin American exports were very expensive abroad and not competitive. For example, with an exchange rate of 5 pesos to the dollar, something that cost 100 pesos to produce would sell for $20 in the United States. But the same product would sell for $33.33 with a 3 to 1 exchange rate. Because of the inability to produce competitive exports and the ability to purchase cheap imports, Latin America had persistent trade deficits.

Since foreign competition was seen as harmful to economic performance, high levels of trade protection emerged. This led to the creation and persistence of inefficient domestic industries incapable of competing in world markets. ISI policies also led to large government sectors, direct government involvement in production, and significant rent-seeking behavior (lobbying the government for special treatment) in order to win contracts and monopoly production rights from the government. Large budget deficits emerged, and high levels of inflation followed. ISI policies led to macroeconomic imbalance, high inflation, uncompetitive industrial production, and declining exports. Despite these problems, Latin American economies generally performed well in the 1950s. Because of the increased state resources devoted to industry, growth rates were high, at times averaging 8 percent per year.

Serious problems with ISI emerged in the late 1950s and early 1960s. In particular, growth rates slowed dramatically as the "easy" part of industrial expansion was completed, and the agricultural sector was in ruin. Though Latin American governments were faced with this poor economic performance, lobbying efforts from those benefiting from the status quo, and poor information and conflicting ideologies over the best path to take, kept Latin America on the same inefficient path for another two decades. During the 1970s the situation worsened. The two world oil shocks considerably worsened the trade deficit for non–oil producers, and oil-producing countries responded to the boom in oil prices by borrowing more to fund industrial and social programs. The price of oil fell as quickly as it had risen in the early 1980s, with the result that the value of oil exports plunged, making it difficult for these countries to purchase the same level of imports. Simultaneously, inflation-fighting macroeconomic policy in the United States substantially increased interest rates. Because of the increased interest payments, the debt load of Latin American nations became too great, and a wave of defaults resulted. In Latin America the 1980s have come to be called the "lost decade." For some countries, notably Mexico, the default was a strong wake-up call indicating that major changes were needed. Mexico implemented a major reform program that culminated in the North American Free Trade Agreement, which is discussed in the next chapter. Other countries, such as Brazil and Argentina, also implemented reforms, with varying degrees of success. What was common in all of them, however, was a smaller role for the state and an opening of markets to foreign competition. Latin America had begun to embrace outward-looking policies like those pursued in East Asia.

It is tempting in hindsight to ask how such inward-looking policies could have been implemented for so long, and how academics, particularly economists, could have supported these protectionist measures. But such questions must be considered within the context of the 1940s and 1950s. Free-trade policies are not guarantees of good economic performance. If an economy's institutional framework leads to high transaction costs, poor performance results regardless of the trade policy pursued. External openness may distort markets less, but they will remain distorted.

If Latin American economies had remained open throughout the post–World War II era, then export sectors would have fared much better and many powerful farmers and business people would have profited. But this would not have led to a thriving internal industrial sector, because, given the costs of transacting in Latin America, it was cheaper to import industrial products. ISI policies explicitly devoted resources and government support to internal industry. Although there were market distortions, and although the farm sector was particularly harmed, many people were better off by being able to obtain manufacturing jobs. The main point is that the complete institutional framework is more powerful than a few of those institutions directed at trade policy. For example, would anyone seriously believe that the United States would be a poor country today if it had adopted ISI policies earlier in the century? There is little doubt that the United States would not be as wealthy, but the impact would have been on the margins. ISI polices in Latin America in the 1940s and 1950s may have been better in the short term than the status quo. The problem was that Latin America did not abandon ISI polices even as market distortions and negative incentives increased.

East Asia's experience differed from Latin America's in four key areas. The East Asia countries undervalued their currencies, avoided excessive protectionist policies, maintained macroeconomic stability, and had a smaller direct role for government. Institutions were put into place that encouraged export production. Firms that achieved strong export sales were rewarded with subsidies and tax breaks. Between 1965 and 1980, despite nearly equal growth rates in the two regions, export growth increased 10 percent per year in Asia, and it declined 1 percent per year in Latin America. Moreover, inflation in East Asia was one-third and debt levels were one-half of those in Latin America.[7] After 1980 the difference in performance is even more striking. East Asian nations were able to respond to and recover from the oil shocks very quickly. Export growth between 1986 and 1991 exceeded 15 percent per year in South Korea, Hong Kong, Singapore, Taiwan, Malaysia, and Thailand, and all of these countries except Malaysia had average annual GDP growth rates of 7 percent or more.[8]

Why did the import substitution model fare poorly in comparison to the export-led model? Let us refer back to our dynamic theory of institutions. Institutions must exist that lead to the process of creative destruction. The incentive system in Latin America certainly failed in this respect. Trade protection from foreign and domestic competition fostered an environment of rent seeking. Firms maximized profits by wining, dining, and bribing government officials instead of producing ever more competitive products through the process of creative destruction. The trade protection that firms received was regarded as secure. It was rare for protection to be given and then revoked a few years later. The government was in the position of having to "pick winners." Since the government decided where special treatment and funding would go, it simultaneously decided which industries it would promote—and hence which would survive, whether or not they were the "fittest" economically. Moreover, the overvalued exchange rate made it impossible for many export sectors to be price competitive. Institutional incentives encouraged neither competition nor technological progress.

In the East Asian model, in contrast, most industrial policy was oriented strictly toward results. Firms that produced results in the form of higher export sales received favorable treatment from the government. Subsidies were seen as temporary rewards for good performance. If a firm received subsidies but exports did not increase shortly thereafter, the subsidies were revoked. This institutional framework did not call for governments to pick individual winners. The governments could wait to see who the winners were, and then reward them accordingly. Moreover, low levels of trade protection meant that Asian firms had to compete in the world economy. The goal of a particular firm was to become the most efficient world producer. This was a highly competitive environment in which the process of creative destruction operated in full force. The subsidies undoubtedly distorted the natural law of comparative advantage, but the distortions were small compared to those in Latin America.

There are other dynamic advantages as well to an outward-looking model. These include an economy better able to take advantage of economies of scale and scope, and the transfer of know-how.[9] *Economies of scale* means that larger-scale operations can be done at lower average costs. In other words, it is cheaper per-unit to produce 10,000 automobiles than it is to produce 200. *Economies of scope* means that gaining expertise in one area lends itself to cost advantages to producing in other areas. For example, a firm that produces stereo sound equipment might find that it is relatively easy to enter the television market. When domestic economies are small, these scale economies are very important. For outward-looking firms, markets are no longer limited to domestic demand but now extend to world demand. Outward-looking models of development also increase the transfer of know-how. In the inward-looking economy, only a narrow range of capital goods is produced. Therefore, only a narrow range of technology is acquired. When economies open up, more capital goods and technology flow in, and workers have incentives to learn and adopt new technology.

Recent economic performance in East Asia suggests that the export-led model is not without its problems. In March 1998 Indonesia's currency was trading at 8,300 rupiahs to the U.S. dollar, about one-fourth of its value on July 1, 1997, when it took just 2,430 rupiahs to purchase a dollar. Likewise, the value of South Korea's currency (the *won*) has declined to about half its July 1997 level. Growth in Indonesia, South Korea, Thailand, and a few other Asian nations has slowed considerably. Banks are saddled with large debts, and many giant corporations are going bankrupt. The IMF has conditionally lent billions of dollars to Indonesia and South Korea to help bail them out. What went wrong?

Economist Paul Krugman explains the Asian crisis with a comparison to a play that has two acts.[10] The first act was a story of the bubble in real-estate and asset prices. Over time, prices of real estate and other assets soared. Two factors in particular contributed to the growth of the bubble. First, there was direct allocation of credit by the government. In South Korea, for example, the government owned key banks and directed funds to certain industries and firms that it targeted. Second, the informal institutions in many Asian nations promoted close ties between government and business. "[T]here was a fuzzy line between what was public and what was private; the minister's nephew or president's son could open a bank and raise money both from the domestic populace and from foreign lenders, with everyone believing that their money was safe. . . . "[11] There was little concern for the soundness of loans or the financial condition of the companies that borrowed funds, as everyone believed that the government would back the lenders if things went wrong. The bubble was inflated further by foreign investment. Foreigners viewed East Asia as a safe haven for funds with high returns.

The second act was the bursting of the bubble. A slump in the semiconductor market and a strengthening of the dollar probably triggered the crisis. Foreign and domestic investors pulled their funds out of Asia, which caused asset prices to plunge. The flow of funds out of the country put downward pressure on Asian currencies, which made the crisis worse by increasing the real debt load of Asian firms holding foreign debt. For example, in Indonesia, as noted earlier, four times as many rupiahs are now required to pay off $1 of debt than before the crisis began. With heavy debt loads and low asset values, many firms declared bankruptcy or defaulted on their payments. Banks were left with bad loans and high foreign debts, and many of them began to fail. In order to avert a larger financial collapse, some Asian governments, with assistance from the IMF, have intervened to bail out the financial sector. The result, however, is slow growth and higher unemployment.

Despite the seriousness of the Asian crisis, we must keep it in perspective. By late 1998 the crisis had not directly spilled over into Japan. Hong Kong and China were not severely affected either. The macroeconomic fundamentals of many Asian nations are still quite sound: Growth is still positive, prices stable, and unemployment low. Severe adjustments are necessary, but this crisis is not on a scale comparable to the 1980s debt crisis in Latin America, because Asian nations are in much better macroeconomic condition. In early 1998 the currencies of Korea, Taiwan, and Thailand stabilized. The worst of the crisis in these countries may be over.

There are at least two changes that the export-led East Asian economies should undertake in response to this crisis. First, governments must reduce their control over their economies, as some already have: "The Finance Ministry in Korea no longer tells the banks whom to lend to, and the Finance Ministry in Japan has lost its capacity to determine the fate of banks and securities houses."[12] Second, relationships among firms must become less important. Much business is done on the basis of loyalty and tradition rather than on price and quality. In an environment of high transaction costs, this may have been a way to make exchanges more secure. But the transaction costs of dealing with outside firms today are relatively low in most of these nations. With large firms going bankrupt and the economy being squeezed with recession, many firms will look for ways to cut costs. Product quality and price will become more important in business dealings.

Developing countries are currently undergoing a great deal of change. Many Latin American nations are moving toward the export-led model, and many Asian nations are moving toward a style of capitalism more like that in the United States. In the next chapter we focus on two developing countries, Mexico and South Korea.

Questions for Discussion

1. What is the informal economy? Give two examples. Why is there a negative correlation between the size of informal economies and per capita GDP?
2. Why does the United States have a very small informal sector?
3. Compare and contrast ISI with export-led policies. Why has the export-led model resulted in relatively better economic performance? Relate your answer to the New Institutional Economics.
4. Many Asian nations recently have run into trouble with currency devaluation, leaving banks and the government saddled with high debts. Growth rates have slowed and unemployment rates are rising. Which formal and informal institutions in these nations contributed to this crisis? Explain. Could such a crisis occur in the United States? Why or why not?

Notes

1. China, a middle-ground case, is discussed in Chapter 11.
2. Hernando de Soto, *The Other Path: The Invisible Revolution in the Third World* (New York: Harper and Row, 1989), p. 12.

3. Hernando de Soto (ibid., p. 60) estimated that there were 90,000 street vendors in Lima, Peru, in 1986.

4. Ibid., pp. 134–135, 144.

5. Ibid., p. 160.

6. For an excellent summary of ISI versus export-led policies, see Sebastian Edwards, *Crisis and Reform in Latin America: From Despair to Hope* (New York: World Bank by Oxford University Press, 1995), chapter 3.

7. Ibid., p. 4.

8. J. Barkley Rosser Jr. and Marina V. Rosser, *Comparative Economics in a Transforming World Economy* (Chicago: Irwin, 1996), p. 452.

9. Rudiger Dornbusch, "The Case for Trade Liberalization in Developing Countries," *Journal of Economic Perspectives*, vol. 6, no. 1 (Winter 1992), pp. 69–85.

10. Paul Krugman, "Asia: What Went Wrong," *Fortune*, March 2, 1998, pp. 32–33.

11. Ibid., p. 32.

12. *New York Times*, "Crisis Pushing Asian Capitalism Closer to U.S.-Style Free Market," January 17, 1998.

10

Mexico and South Korea in Development

The analysis of Mexico and the Republic of Korea, or South Korea, allows us to compare and contrast the divergent models of economic development. Mexico embodies in many ways the ISI model discussed in Chapter 9. It has undergone a series of crises, yet has managed to learn from them and continue down its development path. South Korea turned early toward export promotion and has achieved remarkable success despite the recent economic crisis. This chapter briefly describes the economic history of Mexico from the adoption of ISI policies to the present. It then discusses the rapid transformation of South Korea from the end of the Korean War to the present. The chapter concludes with an institutional comparison of the two nations.

Mexico

Mexico, a nation of 94 million people with a per capita income in 1995 of $6,400 (using purchasing power parity measures), has been ranked by the World Bank as an upper-middle-income country.[1] Mexico is a prime example of a developing economy in reform. Never before has Mexico been so determined to change fundamentally from within. Major institutional changes began after the 1982 debt default, and they continue today. It remains to be seen whether Mexico can stay the course or whether pressures against reform will win out, but there is reason for cautious optimism. The question is whether the spirit of reform carried out on the macroeconomy can be extended to other areas of Mexican society. While much of the discussion that follows focuses on macroeconomic stability, we must remember that stability is only a necessary but not a sufficient condition for good economic performance. It does not by itself guarantee good performance.

The Great Depression and World War II forced Mexico to turn inward for production and demand. This inward-looking policy was formalized in the 1950s with the explicit adoption of import substitution industrialization policies. Mexico raised tariffs and quotas and imposed import license requirements to discourage the importation of consumer goods. The state promoted internal industrialization of consumer goods in the hope that backward linkages would develop so that Mexican firms would be the main suppliers of intermediate inputs throughout the production process. The peso was overvalued to subsidize capital inputs. With the encouragement and resources provided by the government, private investment in Mexico rose from 8 percent to 20 percent of GDP. The average growth rate between 1955 and 1972 was a phenomenal 6.8 percent, and inflation was stable at 3.5 percent.[2] The ISI policies appeared to generate high growth rates and economic stability.

But deep problems lay beneath the surface. First, Mexican firms were not competitive internationally, leaving the economy vulnerable to macroeconomic imbalances such as trade deficits and currency devaluations. Second, the ISI policies generated strong biases against exporters and agriculture. Third, price controls distorted relative prices and kept a lid on inflationary pressures. And fourth, the distribution of income became more unequal as relatively few executives in the inner circle controlled the large domestic industries.

During the early 1970s some thought that despite economic growth in developing countries, the trickle-down policies were not helping the poor much at all. Trickle-down theories advocated giving governments and businesses investment funds in order to increase production and thus create new jobs. The funds disbursed at the top would eventually flow to the poor in the form of wages. As such strategies came to be perceived as ineffective, there was a worldwide push for economic social justice to reduce poverty directly and increase the quality of life for the poor in developing countries. Emphasis was placed on humanitarian aid, health care, and education. With growing unrest from the poor and college students, Mexico began a massive program of public expenditure aimed at reducing poverty. Government expenditures rose from 22 percent of GDP in 1970 to 32 percent of GDP in 1976.[3]

The mid-1970s through the early 1980s was a period of stagnation throughout the world. The first oil shock hit in 1973 when the Organization of Petroleum-Exporting Countries (OPEC) succeeded in significantly restricting output. Much of the world underwent economic recessions and higher-than-normal inflation, but Mexico attempted to avoid recession by borrowing external funds and promoting pro-growth policies. Mexico itself was an oil producer and figured that it could count on higher oil revenues to service the increased debt. Given the massive flow of funds into international banks from OPEC countries, U.S. and other foreign banks were eager to lend funds to Mexico. The growing public expenditures of the Mexican government increased the deficit-to-GDP ratio to 9.9 percent in 1976, and inflation reached 29 percent in 1977.[4] The peso was devalued in August 1976. In that year, Mexico discovered new oil reserves, and oil production increased along with international borrowing. Incredibly, external debt tripled between 1978 and 1982.

Three factors led to an economic crisis in the early 1980s. First, Mexico's economy was dangerously leveraged on the basis of the belief that oil prices would continue to increase. In fact, oil prices peaked in 1981 and declined in every year between 1982 and 1986. Figure 10.1 plots the U.S. dollar price of a barrel of oil against growth rates in Mexico in the 1980s. Though oil was not the only driving force behind the Mexican business cycle, one can observe the correlation between these two variables. The second factor that contributed to the economic crisis was increasing capital flight as the peso became severely overvalued. Mexicans and foreigners exchanged pesos for dollars, and the pressure on the peso increased even more. The third event was monetary policy in the United States. Much of Mexico's debt was denominated in dollars. The Federal Reserve decided to fight inflation aggressively by reducing the money supply. Interest rates tripled. The combination of falling oil revenues, capital flight, and increased interest payments caused Mexico to impose

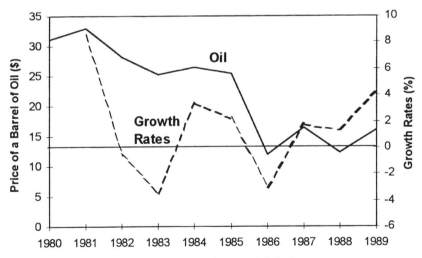

FIGURE 10.1   Price of Oil Versus Growth Rates in Mexico

SOURCES: Oil prices: Energy Information Administration, *Monthly Energy Review* (Washington, DC, April, 1998). Growth rates: INEGI, Sistema de Cuentas Nacionales de Mexico, http://dgcnesyp.inegi.gob.mx/bie.html-ssi.

a moratorium on foreign debt payment in August 1982. Mexico had de-
faulted on its debt.

Crisis brought forth a rapid and dramatic response from the Mexican
government. Indeed, the 1982 debt crisis was the shock that touched off
deep, sustained macroeconomic reform in Mexico. Despite difficulties in
the late 1980s and again in 1995, Mexico has stayed the course. The Program of Immediate Economic Reorganization (PIRE), adopted in December 1982, had three key elements. First, a wage indexation plan tied
wages to expected inflation. Second, the peso was devalued. Third, the
budget deficit was reduced. The result, not surprisingly, was a severe
contraction of the economy and a dramatic rise in poverty. Inflation was
nearly cut in half, from 102 percent in 1983 to 57 percent in 1985. After a
5 percent contraction in real GDP in 1983, the economy grew slightly in
1984 and 1985. But a second series of shocks was to come.

First, a severe earthquake struck Mexico City in December 1985. The
government responded by increasing public expenditures for humanitarian aid. Second, the price of oil plummeted from over US$25 per barrel in
1985 to under $12 per barrel in 1986. Mexico's deficit-to-GDP ratio went
from 6.9 percent in 1985 to 12.8 percent in 1986. The crisis was on again,
and inflation increased to 131 percent in 1987, its highest level in the
1980s. The government responded to this new crisis with another stabilization plan, the Economic Solidarity Pact *(Pacto de Solidaridad Económico).*

The Solidarity Pact was a combination of traditional stabilization policies, price controls, and wage freezes. The truly remarkable aspect of this
pact, however, was the cooperation between the government, labor,
farmer, and business sectors. The pact included fiscal budget cuts in
order to reduce the deficit, devaluation of the peso, privatization, and
trade liberalization. The peso was fixed at 25 pesos to the U.S. dollar,
maximum tariffs were cut from 45 percent to 20 percent, and import license requirements were abolished. In addition, wage and price controls
were imposed to eliminate inertial inflation. The pact was successful. Inflation dropped from 114 percent in 1988 to 20 percent in 1989. Despite
the hardships imposed, Mexico's economy grew between 1987 and 1994.

The capstone to Mexico's commitment to economic reform was the ap-
proval of the North American Free Trade Agreement (NAFTA) in 1993.
Under this agreement most trade barriers between Mexico, Canada, and
the United States will be phased out by the year 2009. Such a trade agreement would have been unthinkable for Mexico just ten years before. Perhaps the largest benefit to Mexico from NAFTA is not the direct benefit
from utilizing its comparative advantage more thoroughly but Mexico's
continued integration into the world economy. NAFTA will force Mexico
to play more by the world rules rather than its own often inefficient rules.

Mexico went through yet another crisis in 1995. As Table 10.1 indicates, the early 1990s were good years for the economy. Inflation was reduced to nearly 7 percent in 1994, and growth rates were strong. The export sector grew by 50 percent between 1990 and 1994. Yet signs of trouble were evident in the trade figures. Though exports were increasing, imports increased even faster. By 1994 the trade deficit had reached alarmingly high levels. Just four months after the inauguration of President Ernesto Zedillo in August 1994, the peso was suddenly and sharply devalued from 3.4 pesos to the U.S. dollar to nearly 6 pesos to the dollar. The devaluation occurred because Mexican reserves fell to such a low level that the government could no longer defend the peso. This led to a loss of confidence in the economy, a sharp drop in the value of Mexican stocks, and the possibility of a massive financial collapse. With a $40 billion loan from the United States government, the Mexican government managed to prevent collapse. After grinding through a depression-like year in 1995, Mexico rebounded strongly in 1996. What did *not* happen after the crisis may be more significant than what did happen. Mexico did not revert back to sustained high inflation rates and large deficits, and the economy remained open to international trade. Macroeconomic reform seems to be well grounded. Perhaps the framework has been set for good economic performance.

TABLE 10.1   Mexico in the 1990s

Year	Growth Rate[a]	Inflation Rate	Budget Deficit[b]	Goods Exports[c]	Goods Imports[c]	Exchange Rate[d]
1991	4.2	18.8	0.4	42,687	49,966	3.02
1992	3.6	11.9	–1.4	46,196	62,130	3.09
1993	2.0	8.0	–0.7	51,885	65,366	3.12
1994	4.4	7.1	0.3	60,879	79,346	3.39
1995	–6.2	52.0	0.2	79,543	72,454	6.45
1996	5.2	27.7	0.1	96,000	89,469	7.60
1997	7.0	15.7	0.7	110,431	109,808	7.92

[a] Percent change in real GDP.
[b] Percent of GDP. Negative values imply a surplus.
[c] Millions of U.S. dollars.
[d] Pesos per U.S. dollar.
SOURCES: Growth rates: Consulate General of Mexico in New York, *Economic Indicators.* Inflation rates: Banco de Mexico: Budget Deficits: Banco de Mexico, *International Financial Statistics,* April 1998. Exports and Imports: 1991–1995 from International Monetary Fund, *International Financial Statistics,* Feb. 1997; 1996–1997 from the Mexican Ministry of Finance and Public Credit. Exchange rates: 1991–1992 from International Monetary Fund, *International Financial Statistics,* February 1997; 1993–1997 from Federal Reserve Board of Governors.

Macroeconomic reform and stability is just one aspect of a nation's institutional framework. Economic performance depends on the level of transaction costs and the incentive systems as determined by the entire network of institutions. Clearly macroeconomic stability is a necessary condition for good economic performance, but much more is needed. The Soviet Union also had a relatively stable macroeconomy during the post–World War II era, but the lack of incentives led to economic stagnation.

Two aspects of Mexican culture that have negative consequences for economic performance stand out. First, there is an emphasis on *machismo*, the romantic vision of the strong, powerful man who exercises power as he sees fit. Such a view fosters the development of corrupt leaders who have little interest in the common good if it conflicts with their own quest for power and prestige. Second, *personalismo* is more important than the rule of law. *Personalismo* is an effective personal relationship with the right people.[5] Law is irrelevant and is considered something to be avoided. Personal satisfaction comes from a spirit of freedom and liberty in doing things "my own way." These attitudes create an environment in which the formal institutions are not respected, and hence enforcement is difficult and transaction costs are high. They also lead to a political system that creates inefficient institutions in order to satisfy the wishes of the leaders.

There are disturbing signs that these attitudes continue in Mexico, unchanged by other structural reforms. Under the rule of the Partido Revolucionario Institucional (PRI), Mexico has had a one-party system since 1929. Such a system invites networking and corruption because there is little political accountability. The government acts much like the single ruler discussed in Chapter 6. It maximizes its own revenue while satisfying those in the party who have influence and power. The result is inefficient institutions that do not create a favorable environment for markets.

Recently there have been challenges to the PRI. For the first time since the PRI took control of the government, Mexico City elected a mayor from an opposition party on July 7, 1997. The PRI also lost a congressional majority. Nonetheless, its dominance in politics continues. Fraud is facilitated in such an environment, because those in power have been there for some time. There is a system of rewarding loyalty and covering for one another, even when one's behavior has been corrupt. This web of networking and corruption appears to be as strong as ever. Three examples can serve to illustrate the point.

First, during the 1994 presidential elections, the PRI's leading candidate, Luis Donaldo Colosio, was assassinated. A shroud of mystery still covers the major aspects of this crime, even though the crime was partially caught on video and a number of people have been arrested. Among those arrested was Raúl Salinas, the brother of former President

Carlos Salinas. He is accused of masterminding the killing. Many people believe that Salinas was only the tip of the iceberg, that many other, higher-level government officials were involved. However, the Mexican government and police have not pursued obvious leads. There is a possibility that Colosio was murdered because he was truly committed to carrying out the reforms that he preached. Colosio posed a threat to corrupt government officials and the leaders of the drug cartels that they supported. An unwritten rule (an informal institution) in Mexico forbids indictment of present and former presidents and high-ranking members of the government. Government officials can be corrupt with the confidence that they will not be charged with crimes. As long as corruption in government is rampant, it is difficult to create an environment in which the rules of the game are clearly spelled out and impartially enforced. Those without the proper connections are shut out.

A second event that illustrates the pervasiveness of corruption in Mexico was the firing of the drug czar, Jose de Jesus Gutierrez Rebollo. Gutierrez was selected for the job by President Zedillo in December 1996. Just two months later, evidence surfaced that he was collaborating with the nation's top drug-trafficking cartel. The fact that the drug cartels are able to make associations with such a high-ranking government official provides some sense of the depth of the problem.

Third, in August 1996 Attorney-General Antonio Lozano Garcia fired 737 federal judicial police because of corruption and ever-growing links between police and drug traffickers. There were accusations that "high-ranking law-enforcement officials . . . were receiving millions of dollars from drug barons in return for safe passage for their lucrative shipments. A rash of killings of high-level investigative police [in 1995 and 1996]— often under circumstances that pointed to other officers as the trigger men—also made decisive action urgent."[6] Mexico City's chief law enforcement official estimated that 50 percent of the city's crime originated in police ranks.[7] The problem is that firing these police officers may simply put them on the street with no jobs but lots of know-how, making many of them definitively part of the criminal establishment.

Mexico has passed through numerous crises in the import substitution phase into a period of relative openness and reform, and it appears that the Mexican government is firmly committed to macroeconomic stability and export-led growth. But Mexico's economy remains inefficient, plagued with high transaction costs. Informal institutions change very slowly. Mexico may have begun the road to true reform in the mid-1980s, but much more needs to be done to change attitudes toward respect for the rule of law and to root out the corruption in the political system if Mexico is to significantly lower transaction costs and create a level playing field for businesses. Mexico may be undergoing a long and slow process of change that continued integration into the world economy will facilitate.

South Korea

As one of the most successful newly industrialized countries, South Korea has become a prime example of successful export-led development policies. To put this performance in perspective, North and South Korea had nearly equal levels of GDP per capita as late as 1975.[8] In 1995 South Korea's per capita GDP was eleven times that of its northern counterpart. The reason for the disparity is the high rate of economic growth that South Korea has achieved. Table 10.2 shows the major macroeconomic indicators by decade for South Korea. These numbers justify calling South Korea's performance an economic miracle.

At the beginning of the twentieth century, Korea was a poor country vulnerable to foreign aggression. In 1905 Russia and Japan fought over control of Korea, and Japan was victorious. In 1910 Japan annexed Korea, controlling it until the end of World War II. Japan devoted many resources to Korea's infrastructure, improved the educational system, and began light industries. But Japan also appropriated the best agricultural land, suppressed Korean language and culture, and killed many in the process. In the 1930s and 1940s Japan neglected Korea, as its resources were devoted to financing the war. Defeat of the Japanese army left the fate of Korea in the hands of the Soviets and the Americans. An agreement was reached in 1945 to temporarily divide Korea along the 38th parallel, with the ultimate goal of reunification in the near future.

Cold War realities prevented a peaceful solution to the Korean division, and by 1948 the Republic of Korea was formally established in the South. The U.S.-backed Syngman Rhee was the first president. In the north, the Democratic People's Republic of Korea was established under Soviet influence. Each side demanded reunification, with its own gov-

TABLE 10.2   South Korea, 1960–1990

	1960s	1970s	1980s
GDP growth[a]	N/A	8.8	9.4
Inflation rate	11.76[b]	15.02	6.05
Export growth[a]	30.1[c]	30.4	13.1

[a] Growth rates are expressed as average annual percentage change.
[b] Data from 1965–1970.
[c] Data from 1966–1970.

SOURCE: Bank of Korea; OECD Economic Outlook No. 61; World Bank, *World Development Report*, 1996, pp. 209, 217.

ernment as the legitimate power. The North Korean army invaded South Korea in 1950. The United Nations responded by sending mostly American troops, who fought the Korean War until an armistice was signed in July 1953. The result was a stalemate. The new military line was the 38th parallel, basically the same as the initial agreement in 1945.

The two Koreas followed very different paths from that point on. Economic growth in South Korea was initially slower than that in the North. South Korea began the postwar era with a large population base of 20 million and little industry. Rice growing and light industry were the primary economic activities. North Korea, in contrast, had about half the population of South Korea and a heavy industrial base.

Syngman Rhee ruled South Korea from 1948 to 1960. His rule had little impact on the economy. The main achievement was a significant land reform begun in 1947 and completed in 1950. Much of the land was taken from a few landlords and redistributed in thousands of smaller plots. The Rhee government was viewed as weak and corrupt, and it adhered to inward-looking protectionist policies. During Rhee's rule, per capita output was stagnant.

In 1961 General Park Chung Hee took control of Korea and ruled until he was assassinated in 1979. Most in 1961 would have predicted more dismal economic performance, but Park made economic reform his top priority and guided the economy through one of the most spectacular growth periods of any nation in history.[9] Park's management style was anything but laissez-faire. But his hands-on approach achieved results when other dictators around the world ruled over increasingly bureaucratic, inefficient economies.

Park created the Economic Planning Board, which was responsible for development planning, budgeting, statistics, price policy, trade regulations, and promotion of foreign investment.[10] The planning function was the most important. Each year beginning in 1962, a five-year plan was developed that targeted key sectors and promoted certain elements in the economy. For example, the first five-year plan emphasized energy production, grain production, and import substitution industries.[11]

The plans were implemented by allocating funds in the budget to accomplish the specified goals. At first the government took on many production projects itself. But with the growth of bureaucracy and significant income losses, production was turned over to the private sector. Firms were not forced to follow the plans, but wise managers saw bigger opportunities and safer investments in those areas that the government actively promoted. Special incentives were offered to firms that produced in the targeted sectors. Among these incentives were tax reductions or exemptions, customs rebates, access to foreign exchange, infant industry protection, and access to credit, usually at low interest rates. Many of the

Korean banks were nationalized; those that remained private were still swayed by Park's agenda. Therefore, firms that produced in the key sectors were basically guaranteed cheap sources of investment funds.

After the first five-year plan, future plans began to emphasize export production. To boost exports, exchange rates were lowered and kept low. The government also rewarded firms that produced results. If a particular firm was successful in meeting previous production targets, then it would be asked to participate in future projects. This facilitated the growth of the *chaebol,* large conglomerates that produce many different types of goods and services. Each *chaebol* is owned by a single family. Some of the largest are Samsung, Lucky-Goldstar, and Hyundai. These *chaebol* were able to take advantage of the expanding Korean economy, and they have grown into enormous entities that sell their export production all over the world. The emphasis on exports encouraged the process of creative destruction abroad even as it stifled competition at home. Korean firms were increasingly externally competitive.

During the 1960s the targeted growth sectors were in food processing, footwear, textiles, cement, plywood, and chemical fertilizers. The 1970s planning emphasis shifted toward heavy industry including machinery, electronics, and shipbuilding. In most cases, the initial objective of the five-year plans was import substitution policy, but the end result was the creation of dynamic organizations that advanced technology and produced products capable of competing in the international economy.

In 1979 Park was assassinated. Korea experienced a recession in 1980. Park's successor was General Chun Doo Hwan, who seized power in 1980 and ruled until 1988, when he voluntarily relinquished power. Chun revised the constitution during his tenure and limited the presidency to a single term, which is now five years. The focus of the 1980s was on the continuation of the economic success that had occurred during the previous fifteen years and on the encouragement of market competition. In other words, the government played a less direct role in the economy under Chun. To the surprise of many, the economic growth continued. As indicated in Table 10.2, the average annual growth rate in the 1980s was 9.4 percent, and export growth continued its surge, growing more than 13 percent per year.

In 1988 power was peacefully and democratically transferred to Roh Tae Woo, and in 1993 Kim Yong-Sam was elected in another peaceful election. Democracy is still tentative in South Korea, but with each passing year it becomes more established. The stable, democratic political institutions make it increasingly difficult for a powerful ruler to change policies quickly, which gives economic policies and institutions more credibility. As Table 10.3 illustrates, the economic miracle has continued through the 1990s. Growth rates have been consistently above 5 percent,

TABLE 10.3   South Korea in the 1990s

Year	Growth Rate[a]	Inflation Rate	Budget Deficit[b]	Exports[c]	Imports[c]	Exchange Rate[d]
1991	9.1	8.91	−2.0	71,870	81,525	733.35
1992	5.1	6.11	−1.5	76,632	81,775	780.65
1993	5.8	4.66	−2.8	82,236	83,800	805.80
1994	8.6	6.03	−3.4	96,013	102,348	806.93
1995	8.9	4.40	−4.0	125,058	135,119	772.69
1996	7.1	4.78	−4.0	129,715	150,339	805.00
1997	5.5	4.38	−3.8	136,164	144,616	950.77

[a] Percent change in real GDP.
[b] Percent of GDP. Negative values imply a surplus.
[c] Millions of U.S. dollars.
[d] Won per U.S. dollar.
SOURCES: Growth rates: Bank of Korea. Inflation rates: Bank of Korea. Budget Deficits: OECD Economic Outlook No. 61, Annex Table 30. Exports and Imports: 1991–1996 from Bank of Korea; 1997 from *International Financial Statistics*, April 1998. Exchange rates: 1991–1992 from *International Financial Statistics*, Feb. 1997; 1993–1997 from Federal Reserve Board of Governors.

inflation rates are relatively low, the currency is stable on foreign exchange markets, the budget has been balanced with small surpluses, and export growth continues to be exceptional. In 1960 exports comprised 4 percent of GDP,[12] and in 1997 the proportion was approximately 33 percent. It is clear that export growth served as the catalyst to South Korea's phenomenal increase in living standards. Its recent history stands in sharp contrast to that of Mexico.

Despite its strong economic performance, South Korea has found itself in the center of the Asian crisis. We discussed in Chapter 9 the main reasons for the Asian crisis. Prices of assets such as real estate were driven to unsustainable levels by government-guided investment and speculation. Finally the bubble burst and asset prices fell as the devaluing domestic currency fled the country. The export-led institutions of South Korea directly contributed to the crisis. Under President Park, the government directly or indirectly allocated nearly all of the investment funds. Those lending the funds perceived that the loans were backed implicitly by the government.

When the bubble burst, the IMF intervened and offered South Korea US$57 billion in financial assistance on the condition that the financial system be restructured to make it more competitive, that trade be opened up, and that rules limiting foreign direct investment be eased.[13] South Korea raised interest rates to slow the outflow of domestic currency. This will undoubtedly slow growth in 1998 and may lead to recession. Many banks may fail, disrupting the process of channeling funds to investors. Therefore, at best, there will be a temporary interruption in the dramatic growth performance that South Korea has experienced since the 1960s.

Mexican and South Korean Development Contrasted

There are two paradoxes in contrasting the economic development of South Korea and Mexico that must be addressed. First, both countries had active, hands-on governmental styles in dealing with the economy. The governments of these countries did more than simply establish the institutional framework and then sit back and let the private organizations do the work. Yet the government control was much more effective in South Korea than in Mexico. Why?

The New Institutional Economics argues that the proper role for government is to create an institutional framework that results in low transaction costs and dynamic competition. The government need not involve itself in direct production activity or in allocating most scarce resources, because the private sector will seize upon profit opportunities and make these decisions for themselves.[14] Much of the history of the United States follows this model. But neither South Korea nor Mexico adhered to this strategy.

The New Institutional Economics also argues that it is very difficult to change paths once a nation has been following a particular path for some time. Path-dependence, informal institutions, and competing ideologies account for this. Therefore, the theory seems to advocate conflicting advice in some historical cases. Should government take a back seat and simply provide the proper institutional framework, or should it take a more proactive role and coordinate production directly? The correct answer is that it depends. If the path-dependent forces overwhelm a nation's ability to make the necessary institutional changes, then more direct government action may be necessary until private organizations exist and function well enough that they can respond to the right incentives. It is likely that Mexico and South Korea could not or would not change their institutional frameworks in the early 1950s to reduce transaction costs and create positive dynamic incentives. Moreover, in the case of South Korea, there were few organizations or educated laborers after the Korean War who were able to take advantage of a low-transaction-cost environment even if the government had been able to provide one. Thus both countries needed a forceful "push" to take their economies down another path. Direct government action provided that push.

In both cases, direct government intervention resulted in sustained economic growth. Mexico had a per capita growth rate of 2.8 percent between 1940 and 1954 and a growth rate of 3.4 percent between 1954 and

1970. Between 1925 and 1940, though, growth had been stagnant in Mexico.[15] The push to industrialize boosted the economy throughout most of the 1960s. The government involvement, however, led to a growing bureaucracy, budget deficits, and inefficient organizations. Moreover, corruption and abuse of power increased as government officials gained more control over the economy. The flaw in the Mexican government's strategy was not the initial expansion that supported ISI but the government's inability or unwillingness to reduce its direct role in the economy once industries were established. Private industries were not growing on their own, because of the high transaction costs, but once the industries were in place the institutional framework needed to progress in order to lower transaction costs and promote competition. Instead, path-dependence and an ideology based on dependency theory led Mexico further down the path of large government involvement and trade protection. What Mexico should have done is to reduce direct government involvement and remove trade barriers as the industrial sector grew.

South Korea also had extensive direct government involvement throughout the Park regime. In the years after the Korean War, there was little choice. The private organizations and labor force were not equipped to produce complex industrial products. The government took on the role of producing directly and encouraged the formation of organizations to produce in the targeted sectors. However, the South Korean government learned early on that direct government production led to inefficiencies and costly bureaucracies. Therefore, emphasis shifted to private production as opposed to nationalization of industries. Moreover, after the first five-year plan, the Economic Planning Board allocated resources on the basis of export production. Firms were required to perform competitively in order to receive further favorable treatment from the government. Though corruption and abuse of power were present, they did not dominate or dictate economic policy. The *chaebol* may have had considerable influence on the government, but that influence was not sufficient to justify continued favorable treatment if production stagnated. In the 1980s, once the industrial foundation of South Korea was firmly in place, General Chun took the wise step of limiting direct government activity in the economy. Earlier, President Park had facilitated the development of the organizations and labor force necessary to function well in a capitalist economy. Now it was time for the government to reduce its direct role in the economy and let the private firms compete more among themselves for resources and profit opportunities—which is precisely what South Korea did in the 1980s.

This does not mean that the South Korean government was perfect. The government made many mistakes and sometimes picked industries to support that did not perform well. They channeled funds into unprofitable ventures and left the economy vulnerable to the Asian crisis. Moreover, the *chaebol* may be a source of fantastic export production, but the oligopolist structure also limits domestic competition. South Korean consumers pay higher prices for many products than foreign consumers who purchase the exports. This lack of domestic competition will likely cause some hardships in South Korea in the near future. Nevertheless, the South Korean government was able to reduce its intervention when it was no longer necessary. Moreover, the Korean firms were not able to establish the cozy relationship with the government that the Mexican firms had. Economic performance carried more weight than political connections.

The second paradox in contrasting the Mexican and the South Korean development strategies is that the import substitution polices followed in each country had radically different results. South Korea essentially adopted import substitution strategies that led to the formation of dynamic organizations that became the sources of new technologies and dynamic export growth. In contrast, import substitution policies in Mexico led to technological stagnation and lackluster export growth. What accounts for the difference?

As with the first paradox, the answer lies in the dynamic incentives under which the organizations operated. Mexico's version of import substitution was imposed rigidly, with trade protection guaranteed without regard to economic efficiency. Political connections, not economic performance, assured continuing trade protection. Moreover, implementation of import substitution in Mexico led to an inflated exchange rate. The strong currency lowered the price of key intermediate inputs necessary to produce the final manufactured goods, but the overvalued peso also raised the price of exports abroad and made Mexican firms uncompetitive internationally. Therefore, import substitution polices focused on internal domestic demand with little concern for international competition. The domestic competition was limited as well, because the Mexican government favored certain domestic producers. Many producers had virtual monopolies. With little domestic or foreign competition, the process of creative destruction was absent and technology stagnated.

The implementation of import substitution was very different in South Korea. In the institutional arrangement with Korean firms, trade protection was temporary, and firms' rewards depended on results as measured by exports. Once the industry matured, firms were expected to thrive internationally. If not, resources would be diverted to firms that were more successful. To avoid trade deficits, the South Korean government undervalued the currency, thus promoting export sales. Import substitution policies in South Korea were not designed to permanently protect Korean producers from competition, but to give them temporary breathing room so that they could compete internationally. Exchange rate policy reinforced this. Therefore, the process of creative destruction operated in Korea primarily because of international competition.

One could argue that the South Korean government did not need to protect these infant industries to begin with, that they could have survived on their own with private financing. Indeed, some of them could have. But early trade protection significantly lowered the risks to firms expanding into new areas. Moreover, since the government controlled credit allocation, private financing may have been impossible without explicit government targeting of an industry. In essence, the South Korean government picked industries that it thought would be successful. Sometimes the government made mistakes. In the late 1970s, for example, the plan emphasized the production of heavy machinery, machine tools, power generators, and telecommunications equipment. None of these sectors was particularly successful, and the government had to bail them out when heavy losses resulted.[16] These losses could have been avoided with less direct government involvement. Overall, however, the import substitution policies of the South Korean government encouraged enough productive behavior to absorb these losses. Import substitution succeeded in South Korea and ultimately failed in Mexico because the Korean protection was oriented toward becoming internationally competitive, whereas in Mexico the import substitution institutions failed to promote competition internally or externally. Hence Mexican living standards stagnated while those in South Korea rose quickly.

Questions for Discussion

1. Describe the domestic and international events that led to the oil crisis in Mexico. How did Mexico respond to this crisis? Do you think Mexico is on the right path now?

2. Why do you think the oil crisis disrupted Latin American economies so profoundly in the 1980s, whereas the East Asian nations seemed to adjust rather easily?

3. What are two reasons why import substitution policies were more effective in South Korea than in Mexico?

4. How has South Korea's economy performed lately? What were the significant adjustments that they made?

5. Does the Asian crisis imply that the U.S. model of capitalism is superior? What aspects of the South Korean economy might be better than those in the United States? Should the economic institutions of South Korea change to look more like those in the United States? Explain.

Notes

1. World Bank, *World Development Report*, 1997, p. 215. Mexico's per capita GDP is 24 percent of that in the United States.

2. Nader Nazmi, *Economic Policy and Stabilization in Latin America* (New York: M. E. Sharpe, 1996), p. 88.

3. Ibid., p. 90.

4. Ibid., p. 91.

5. Lawrence E. Harrison, *Underdevelopment Is a State of Mind: The Latin American Case* (Lanham, MD: Center for International Affairs, Harvard University, and Madison Books, 1985), p. 146–147.

6. *Christian Science Monitor*, "Massive Firing of Police in Mexico May Turn Some into New Criminals," August 23, 1996.

7. Ibid.

8. Some have argued that the North Korean estimates were inflated.

9. Japan still outperformed Korea, with even faster growth rates between 1950 and 1990.

10. Jon Woronoff, *Asia's "Miracle" Economies* (New York: M. E. Sharpe, 1986), p. 97.

11. J. Barkley Rosser Jr. and Marina V. Rosser, *Comparative Economics in a Transforming World Economy* (Chicago: Irwin, 1996), p. 446.

12. Woronoff, *Asia's "Miracle" Economies*, p. 113.

13. *New York Times*, "Economic Scene: South Korea Facing Difficult Economic Choices," December 18, 1997.

14. The major exception to this rule is the government's role in providing public goods such as national defense. If national defense is left to the private sector, it will be underproduced relative to the efficient level, because private firms cannot exclude nonpaying consumers from enjoying the benefits of national security.

15. Rosser and Rosser, *Comparative Economics in a Transforming World Economy*, p. 418.

16. Woronoff, *Asia's "Miracle" Economies*, p. 111.

11

China in Transition and Development

China

With a population of 1.2 billion, China is the largest nation in the world. Despite rapid economic growth since 1980, it remains a poor country. In 1995 China's per capita GDP was not quite 11 percent of that of the United States.[1] China is not easily categorized as a transition economy or a developing economy, for it is both. China has undergone profound changes in its economic institutions—enough to be classified as a transition economy—yet its political and social institutions remain largely intact. Therefore, it can also be classified as a developing economy, one that has made rapid progress in increasing its living standards in recent years. China is the greatest survivor of the collapse of Communism around the world. However, it has introduced widespread economic decentralization and permitted the growth of private markets in order to survive economically. This combination of political dictatorship and economic liberalization results in a political economic system referred to as a *socialist market economy*.

China is a country composed of provinces. Mainland China, Hong Kong, and Taiwan constitute the *Chinese economic area*. Hong Kong was taken from the Chinese in the mid-1800s by the English in the Opium Wars. It prospered as a British colony until July 1, 1997, when it was turned over to China. Taiwan's status is less clear. When Communists drove out the Nationalist government in 1949, the Nationalists fled to Taiwan, where they adopted capitalist institutions and have had a semblance of independence since then. However, while Taiwan views itself as a separate nation, mainland China sees Taiwan as a renegade province that may need to be reined in one day. China has successfully pressured other nations, including the United States, to stop extending to Taiwan recognition as a separate entity.

China's recent history can be categorized by distinct periods of change. In this chapter we review the institutional changes that took place in mainland China and the consequences that followed for China's economy. We will see that China's economic performance since 1980 was fundamentally affected by the set of formal institutions adopted by Chinese leaders. We also examine the impact that Hong Kong's recent merger with mainland China is likely to have on Hong Kong's economic performance.

Mainland China

China's history is linked with cycles of rising and falling dynasties. Some of the more important ones include the Yuan (1276 to 1367), the Ming (1368 to 1644), and the Qing (1645 to 1911).[2] In 1911 the Qing dynasty was overthrown and China declared itself a republic. There was political unrest until 1928, when Chiang Kai-shek led the Nationalists to power. The 1930s was a decade of war, famine, and economic difficulty. The Communist party increased in strength and drove out the Nationalists, who fled to Taiwan in 1949. Mao Zedong led the country.

The period from 1949 to 1957 was one of consolidation of state power, modeled after the Soviet system. Land reforms were carried out that converted all farms into collectives. Property rights to farmland were seized by the state. The same pattern was followed for businesses. By 1957 nearly all industry in China was state owned or formed into collectives. Mao then implemented a series of radical polices that broke with Soviet experience and caused tension between the two nations.

The first of these was the two-year period from 1958 to 1960, which is known as the Great Leap Forward. Soviet-style growth had taken place by heavy investment in capital to create large-scale industries. This seemed inappropriate to China's situation, because it favored urban development over rural development. But China was overwhelmingly a rural economy. Moreover, the process of capital accumulation was slow, and the nation had an abundance of labor resources that were underutilized. Mao's vision was that the masses of peasants would generate rapid growth in the economy by the development of labor-intensive investment projects spread throughout the countryside. The excess labor resources could be put to use without the need for large capital investments. In agriculture, communes were established. Peasants not only lost their land and capital, but also they were forced from their homes so that they would be mobile, ready to relocate to another area if called upon. Industrial investments focused on small-scale production processes based in the communes. The largest of these investments was the construction of millions of backyard furnaces that produced steel. Other projects included machine shops, cement production, and food processing.[3]

The Great Leap Forward was an economic and humanitarian disaster. Despite an initial surge in output in 1958, much of which was of poor quality and hence unusable, the trend soon reversed. Industrial output declined in 1960 and plummeted in 1961. As bad as the industrial performance was, agricultural performance was far worse. Many peasants slaughtered livestock in protest of the formation of communes. Blurred property rights in the commune system left farmers with little incentive to produce. There was a weak relationship between work effort and economic reward. These inefficiencies and a series of natural disasters led to the worst famine ever in history. Somewhere between 15 and 30 million people died from starvation between 1958 and 1961. There has probably never been a series of peacetime institutional and organizational changes that resulted in such death and destruction as the Great Leap Forward.

Mao retreated from these policies and accepted blame for the disaster. The level of accountability in communes was lowered from the brigade to the production team. In other words, communes operated more as if they were collectives. In the mid-1960s industrial and agricultural output grew strongly. But Mao struck again in 1966 with the Great Proletarian Cultural Revolution. This was Mao's attempt to establish pure communism and weed out all strains of Western thought. Mao hoped that public interest would rise above individual need. During the Cultural Revolution, thousands of intellectuals, bureaucrats, and students were sent to the countryside by train for "reeducation." Many were dropped off in the rural areas with no place to stay and no job. Moreover, the farmers who had to support them did not happily receive them.

Output fell between 1966 and 1968 because of the disruption from the Cultural Revolution. In response, the official Revolution was halted, and five-year plans were reintroduced. In 1976 Mao died. After an internal struggle for power, Deng Xiaoping became China's leader and began a series of institutional reforms, the consequences of which are still felt today.

Deng's goal was to modernize China's ailing economy. He implemented the Four Modernizations Program, which focused on the four areas of agriculture, industry, science and technology, and national defense. In agriculture, farming organizations were again grouped into collectives, and the *household responsibility system* was introduced. Though land was still held by the state, it was divided into small plots and contracted out to be privately farmed. In addition, a two-tier price system was established. Under this arrangement, a farmer had to deliver a certain amount of agricultural output to the state at a fixed price. Any production in excess of the state quota could be sold in the free market. Over time, the government reduced the share of production under quota and allowed more foodstuffs to be traded on the market. These institutional reforms sharpened the profit motive for the farmers. The result was a surge in agricultural productivity. Per capita food production rose 20 percent between 1980 and 1985.[4]

Industry reforms were also implemented to greatly increase the private sector. There are three basic types of industry ownership in China: state-owned enterprises (SOEs), collective enterprises, and private enterprise. In 1978 the state-owned sector accounted for over three-quarters of industrial production; in 1994 the proportion was 43 percent.[5] In the 1980s the government decentralized oversight of many SOEs and, as it had in agriculture, set up a two-tier price system in which firms can sell any surplus beyond a minimum state quota. Responsibility for managing many SOEs was passed to local governments. Unlike in other transition economies, SOEs are still projected to play an important role in China's production. But the growth of collectives and private firms has diminished the relative importance of the SOEs.

Town and village enterprises (TVEs) are a novel type of organization that arose from enterprise reform in the 1980s. These are enterprises that are collectively owned, usually by local governments. They represent a middle ground between state-owned and private firms. The local government acts like a holding company, reinvesting profits in existing firms or financing new ones. A portion of the profits also goes to local infrastructure.[6] Despite the inefficiencies that are often associated with common property rights, TVEs have performed remarkably well. In 1994 they accounted for 31 percent of China's GDP. Capital-labor ratios in TVEs are only 25 percent of those in the state sector, yet their labor productivity is 80 percent of the state enterprise level. The success of these collective organizations is attributed to at least two factors. First, there is a strong kinship link among Chinese villagers that encourages responsibility to the group. This informal institution acts as a constraint on incentives for individual gain. Second, limited government budgets impose hard budget constraints and fiscal discipline on TVEs. Local governments rely on profits generated from TVEs. Unsuccessful enterprises quickly become a drain on government budgets and are unsustainable.[7] TVEs are clearly driven by the communal values of rural villages. Such an organizational structure would be nearly impossible to implement in a country as individualistic as the United States.

The final type of industrial ownership is private enterprise. This form is still relatively modest in China, accounting for no more than 10 percent of industrial production. However, one must remember that before 1980 there were no private enterprises in China. Moreover, this sector is growing very quickly and is sure to become much more important in the near future.

China has been very successful in attracting foreign investment. Between 1989 and 1995 it far outpaced every transition economy except Hungary.[8] Indeed, in 1997 China attracted a record US$45 billion in foreign direct investment.[9] China facilitated foreign investment by the establishment of *special economic zones* (SEZs)—specially selected ports that have relaxed rules for foreign transactions. The first four of these areas were designated in 1980, and fourteen more were selected in 1984. Foreign investors get preferential tax treatment, flexible wage and labor policies, and less red tape. These SEZs have experienced phenomenal growth in recent years and have been the dynamism behind China's surge in exports. Exports have increased 250 percent since 1990. Chinese firms have had increasing access to foreign exchange, though it is still restricted by the state.

Recently China has been pressing for membership in the World Trade Organization. Membership would require that China's trade rules conform with the policies of the General Agreement on Tariffs and Trade (GATT). Three key institutions need to be changed. First, foreign companies currently operating in China must export virtually everything they produce so that goods do not compete with China's domestic SOEs. Second, foreign companies have no trading rights. For example, multinationals must negotiate permission to import goods necessary as inputs in the production process. Third, foreign companies must bring in and maintain large amounts of foreign currency, and they must use high levels of local content in their production processes. China has indicated a willingness to make changes in these institutions, which is a sign of how far China has come in its outward orientation.

China's growth rates have been among the highest in the world since 1980, averaging 10 percent per year. Table 11.1 lists the key economic indicators for China in the 1990s. China is no longer among the lowest ranks of poor countries. Change in China's economic institutions has led to this economic performance. Under Mao, economic organizations had few incentives to engage in the process of creative destruction, but the market reforms under Deng have changed this.

Despite Communist control, recent reform of the political system in China has made it more conducive to producing efficient economic institutions. Recall that market-preserving federalism is a political system that encourages the development of the property rights that are necessary for markets to function well. Market-preserving federalism requires a hierarchy of government and institutional durability of that hierarchy. It also requires that subnational governments have primary authority over the economy, that all levels of government face hard budget constraints, and that a higher level government establish a common market. When these five conditions are met, lower-level governments compete with one another to create environments conducive to business. Gabriella Montinola and her colleagues have argued that China's version of market-preserving federalism is imperfect but provides enough incentives to allow markets to grow.[10]

TABLE 11.1   China's Key Economic Indicators

Year	Growth Rate[a]	Inflation Rate	Budget Deficit[b]	Exports[c]	Exchange Rate[d]
1990	3.9	1.6	0.75	62,091	4.78
1991	8.0	3.0	0.94	71,910	5.32
1992	13.6	5.4	0.89	84,940	5.51
1993	13.4	13.0	0.58	90,970	5.76
1994	11.8	21.7	1.23	121,047	8.62
1995	10.2	17.0	1.00	148,797	8.35
1996	9.7	8.3	N/A	151,000	8.34
1997	8.8	2.8	N/A	N/A	8.32

[a] Percent change in real GDP.
[b] Percent in GDP.
[c] Millions of U.S. dollars.
[d] Yuan per U.S. dollar.
SOURCES: Growth rates: 1990–1995 from World Bank, *World Development Report*, 1996, pp. 172–174; 1996 from *Transitions Newsletter*, vol. 8(1), Feb. 1997; 1997 from *Transitions Newsletter*, vol. 9(1), Feb. 1998. Inflation rates: 1990–1995, *World Development Report*, pp. 172–174; 1996–1997 from *International Financial Statistics*, April 1998. Budget Deficits: 1990–1995 from *International Financial Statistics*, Feb. 1997. Exports: China Economic Information Network, 1997 Yearbook, www.cei.gov.cn/indexe.html. Exchange rates: 1990–1995, *International Financial Statistics*, Feb. 1997; 1996–1997 from Board of Governors, Federal Reserve System.

Economic authority is decentralized because local governments, rather than the central government, control many SOEs. Reforms in the 1980s accelerated this trend. "By 1985 state-owned industrial enterprises controlled by the central government accounted for only 20 percent of the total industrial output from such enterprises at or above township level."[11] Economic activity in the SEZs is also decentralized; local governments have authority, for example, to approve foreign investment projects.

A hard budget constraint is achieved by a fiscal revenue-sharing system between any two adjacent levels of government. Lower-level government contracts with upper-level government on the total amount of taxes and profits that will be remitted; the lower-level government keeps the rest.[12] This revenue-sharing arrangement provides incentives for local governments to prosper, because they are able to keep the additional profits. Township and village governments in particular operate under a hard budget constraint, because they have no authority to regulate the market. This may partially account for the successful growth of TVEs. It also accounts for the fact that in 1989 about 3 million TVEs went bankrupt or were taken over by other TVEs.[13] Nevertheless, the banking system has created a loophole in the budget constraint. Local governments have substantial influence over credit allocation in their jurisdictions, and they use that influence to direct credit to local SOEs. However, the local governments also have the power to decide whether or not the enterprise must pay back the loan. Therefore, the local enterprises do not always have to suffer the consequences of their actions.

Like the hard budget constraint, the common market condition is not perfectly satisfied either in China. Labor and capital mobility are imperfect, and local governments have erected substantial trade barriers. These limitations imply that subnational governments do not have to provide a positive market environment, because they can protect themselves from the capital and labor outflow that would normally occur. Moreover, if another jurisdiction produces a superior product, the local government can block its import by imposing tariffs or quotas. Nevertheless, there is a clear trend toward more factor mobility, as many migrant workers are flowing to economically vibrant cities. Over time we would expect to see more pressure for openness as residents of particular regions press their governments to adopt policies that have been implemented successfully elsewhere.

How durable is the power of the local governments? There is reason to believe that their power has become more durable in recent years because of the success of economic reforms. First, the economic growth of local provinces has given those regions independent sources of revenue and political support. The authority of national leaders has weakened as the authority of local leaders has risen. Second, the ability of the central government to monitor and control local economic behavior has weakened because of the rapid growth of these economies. Third, an attempt at economic recentralization by the national government would be costly and would strain the government's fiscal capacity. It would be costly because production would fall in the local economies and unemployment would rise. Thus the government would be faced with declining tax revenues and increased need for social expenditures.[14] Though market-preserving federalism is certainly not complete in China, enough of the conditions are satisfied that institutions are being created that encourage and preserve markets. This explains how China can achieve and sustain rapid growth in the context of a socialist government with little regard for private property.

Despite these successes, difficult issues remain that could spell trouble for China down the road. First, political stability is kept by force. As the 1989 Tiananmen Square incident showed, the government is repressing growing democracy movements in the country. As Chinese citizens experience more economic liberty, they will need and desire more political liberty. A Chinese entrepreneur who has taken many financial risks, for example, will not like state interference that negatively affects his or her business. Over time, such entrepreneurs will demand more political accountability. The economic freedom and growth in consumerism also instills more and more Western ideals and values into Chinese society. It may be only a matter of time before continuing economic freedom and political repression become incompatible.

A second hindrance to China's development is the high level of transaction costs, in part because of corruption. Corruption is rampant in China, and businesses often have no recourse when a government official extorts revenue. The legal system is not impartial but run by the Communist party leaders. More effort seems to be put into political repression than into enforcing contracts. For now, corruption seems to be controllable by the government, unlike the situation in Russia. But the decentralization that has occurred in the Chinese government may allow corruption to blossom.

Transaction costs are high in China for another reason. There is an informal institution called *guanxi*, which means "relationships." *Guanxi* is the way business and political negotiations are carried out in China. The Chinese do not trust legalistic negotiations; they prefer to develop personal friendships with individuals who will then be obligated to them. A trusted friend is much safer than uncertain rules and legal systems. The Chinese begin negotiations by establishing informal relationships with their partners. Then they use that friendship to manipulate negotiations in their favor. When an agreement has been reached, enforcement is not guaranteed. The Chinese very often demand renegotiation of the contract terms. *Guanxi* is an ongoing relationship that is constantly used to improve bargaining positions.

Among the Chinese, *guanxi* is an informal institution that lowers transaction costs in the absence of a reliable, well-functioning legal system. However, it invites corruption, discrimination, and closed-door negotiations. If a business person does not have the right *guanxi*, he or she is shut out of the market regardless of the product's quality and price. To Western society, *guanxi* is a frustrating institution that leads to high transaction costs. Western businesses like to negotiate the terms of a contract, make a deal, and then move on to other issues, leaving the legal system to enforce disagreements. This is not possible in China. Western firms must spend enormous amounts of time cultivating relationships with the right people in China. Boeing has had a great deal of experience in building *guanxi*. With billions of dollars of airplane orders on the horizon, Boeing has spent a few billion dollars "courting" Chinese politicians and businesses. "Over the past two years, Boeing has invested $150 million to beef up sales, maintenance, and training operations across China. . . . Since 1993, Boeing has taken more than 1,000 mainland mechanics and pilots to the U.S. for training. Last year alone, it hosted 3,500 Chinese visitors in Seattle."[15] This type of negotiating may be possible for the large firms with deep pockets and a long time horizon, but it shuts out many smaller firms that have to make quick returns on investments. As China integrates more and more into the Western world, *guanxi* will become more of an obstacle for foreign trade.

The third main difficulty facing China is the condition of its banking system. The four main commercial banks are technically insolvent.[16] The banking system is saddled with bad debt and nonperforming loans. Like other Asian nations, the government has been highly involved in allocating credit with little concern for the ability of the enterprises to repay their loans. A large part of the bad loans were policy loans, initiated by the government to enable state companies to provide housing, schools, and hospitals.[17] Chinese banks are also heavily exposed to real estate loans with declining market values. The Chinese government recently announced intentions to recapitalize the four largest banks, and it is giving local banks some authority to adjust interest rates according to the risk profile of the borrower. Despite the similarities of China's banking system with that in South Korea and other Asian nations, many believe that China will not succumb to the Asian crisis. This is because most of its foreign investment is long-term and cannot flee the country during a wave of panic. China also has large trade surpluses and enormous foreign exchange reserves, sufficient to be able to fend off currency devaluation.

The final key problem for China is its environment. Beijing already has the dirtiest air in the world. Economic growth is driven by burning dirty coal, leading to disastrous pollution problems. "China's heavy reliance on coal, along with its inefficient and wasteful patterns of energy use, will make it the largest single producer of climate-warming carbon dioxide by the second or third decade of the next century."[18] The problem is widespread. "Even if China improved the efficiency of its electric power plants, much of the coal burned in China is consumed in small industrial and municipal boilers and in millions of cooking stoves and household heaters, for which no alternative fuels are currently available."[19] Currently China is not willing to sacrifice growth for a cleaner environment. As its economy grows, the opportunity cost of cleaning up may not be as high. But for now, there seems little that can be done to prevent the increased environmental degradation.

China has grown tremendously in recent years. Changes in formal economic institutions are responsible for most of this growth. China's recent history is an excellent example of the profound impact that a nation's institutional framework has on economic performance. It remains to be seen whether China can continue to develop its institutions to deal with political liberalization, high transaction costs, and environmental damage.

China has recently undergone another profound change: the transition of Hong Kong from British control to Chinese control.

The Incorporation of Hong Kong

Hong Kong is one of the world's leading financial centers. It is a bustling, thriving province of 6.1 million people, and has a GDP per capita of over US$21,000. Hong Kong was taken from China by the British in the Opium Wars of 1839–1842. In 1898 the two nations signed a ninety-nine-year lease of Hong Kong that expired July 1, 1997, ending Hong Kong's colonial era and establishing Hong Kong as a Special Administrative Region (SAR) of China. The transfer of power from Britain to China has created a remarkable experiment in economic history: the merger of a democratic, capitalist republic with a Communist government. This is certainly one of the few times in history in which decolonization has led to an initial reduction in political freedom. Hong Kong's formal institutions are now set (within limits) by the People's Republic of China. It remains to be seen what impact this merger will have on the economic performance of Hong Kong and China.

China has agreed to the principle of "one country, two systems." As part of the transition negotiations, China adopted the Basic Law of 1990 as a constitution for Hong Kong, which stipulates fifty years of status quo in Hong Kong; there is to be no significant institutional change during that period. Yet no one believes that this will be the case. Change will prevail. The question is, what type of change? If China honors the Basic Law, certain institutional changes are off-limits. For example, Hong Kong will retain its own currency (the Hong Kong dollar), its own monetary policy, and control over foreign transactions. China is not allowed to impose its own exchange controls or to restrict trade. Hong Kong is and will remain a member of the World Trade Organization. Its products are to be accounted for separately from those of the mainland.

In sum, formal economic institutions may not be affected much at all. In fact, as we have seen, China's formal economic institutions are becoming more capitalistic each day. China undoubtedly perceives that making sure that Hong Kong continues to perform well would be in China's best interest, because Hong Kong serves as an important source of capital for the mainland. Moreover, it is now China's most visible and economically successful region. The West will react to any missteps by the mainland swiftly and negatively. Indeed, throughout the Asian crisis, the mainland honored the Basic Law and did not intervene in Hong Kong's autonomy.

The Taiwanese are watching Hong Kong's progression closely. Although the mainland considers Taiwan a renegade province, many people in Taiwan wish to reunite with China if certain freedoms and guarantees can be made. Hong Kong thus serves as an important experiment for Taiwan. If the "one country, two systems" policy fails in Hong Kong, the possibility of negotiating a peaceful merger with Taiwan will diminish considerably. Hence China is constrained by the Basic Law, by a desire to maintain good foreign relations, and by a desire to resolve peacefully its differences with Taiwan.

The real changes in Hong Kong will be in political and informal institutions. China has given early signals of how it will change political institutions. On the very day that Hong Kong was transferred to China, the elected Hong Kong legislature was replaced by a Beijing-appointed body headed by Tung Chee-hwa. Tung has indicated that rights to organize and to protest publicly will be curtailed. Hong Kong will require that all organizations register with the police, and the government will have the power to ban any organization that it perceives as a threat to national security. Moreover, organizations wishing to protest must seek permission from the police seven days in advance. The police will have the power to ban protests for national security reasons.[20]

China's informal institutions will also filter into Hong Kong's economy. The main concern is that corruption will greatly increase. "Fully 84 percent of Hong Kong's people believe that Chinese officials are corrupt, according to a poll conducted by the Hong Kong Transition Project. . . . And 55 percent of Hong Kong's people believe that corruption will become more common under Chinese rule."[21] The worry is that China's informal institutions will cross into Hong Kong along with the mainland firms. Hong Kong has an Independent Commission Against Corruption that successfully cracks down on all kinds of corruption. Tung has said that he will remove the word "Independent" from the commission's name. This signals the intention of China's government to become more involved in the commission's activities. The impartiality of the judiciary system also may suffer. Many question whether the judiciary will be able to resist political pressure from Beijing. Moreover, the highest appeals court is being replaced by a five-member Court of Final Appeal. The justices of this court will be named by Tung.[22] If China's system of corruption and *guanxi* infiltrate Hong Kong's rule of law, transaction costs will rise and economic performance will suffer. The important criterion for success will be whom one knows rather than economic efficiency.

Despite the promise of fifty years of "status quo," the integration of Hong Kong with China will bring change. Some believe, however, that Hong Kong will have a larger impact on the mainland than the mainland will have on Hong Kong, for two reasons. First, under the "one country, two systems" principle, those living under political repression will resent that their countrymen in Hong Kong can openly exercise rights such as criticism of government officials. Pressure may mount in China to give equal rights to all. Second, China may be less afraid of democracy as it observes the successful performance of Hong Kong's political and economic institutions.

The key to a successful transition is to retain Hong Kong's institutional framework. If China changes the formal institutions too radically, or if the informal institutions of corruption and *guanxi* infiltrate Hong Kong, then economic performance will suffer. On the eve of transition, the evidence indicated that people in Hong Kong do not expect big changes. Kenneth Kasa studied the financial markets in Hong Kong leading up to the transition, theorizing that concerns about the transition should be manifested in Hong Kong's stock and bond markets.[23] In particular, the gap between Hong Kong and U.S. interest rates should increase, because of the increased risk of holding assets in Hong Kong, and the stock market should become more volatile. Evidence up to the date of transition showed no increase in the interest rate gap or any break in trend in the stock market. Investors in Hong Kong's financial markets do not expect radical change. Time will tell whether they are correct.

Questions for Discussion

1. Describe the main economic reforms that China implemented in the late 1970s and 1980s. Why were they successful?

2. Can China succeed in the long run as a Communist nation? How will the growth of markets conflict with the lack of political freedom in China?

3. Will China's incorporation of Hong Kong have a greater impact on China or on Hong Kong? Explain.

4. Define *guanxi*. Explain the paradox of how *guanxi* seemingly lowers transaction costs within China, but raises transaction costs in exchanges with foreigners.

Notes

1. World Bank, *World Development Report* (New York: Oxford University Press, 1997), pp. 214–215.

2. J. Barkley Rosser Jr. and Marina V. Rosser, *Comparative Economics in a Transforming World Economy* (Chicago: Irwin, 1996), p. 360.

3. Martin C. Schnitzer, *Comparative Economic Systems*, 7th ed. (Cincinnati: South-Western Publishing, 1997), p. 335. The industrial policy has been called "the steel mill in every backyard" policy.

4. Ibid., p. 353.

5. Ibid., p. 347.

6. *World Development Report*, 1996, p. 51.

7. Ibid.

8. Ibid., p. 64.

9. "China's Economy at a Crossroads," *Transition Newsletter*, vol. 9, no. 1 (February 1998).

10. Gabriella Montinola, Yingyi Qian, and Barry R. Weingast, "Federalism, Chinese Style: The Political Basis for Economic Success in China," *World Politics*, vol. 48 (October 1995), pp. 50–81.

11. Ibid., pp. 61–62.

12. Ibid., p. 63.

13. Ibid., p. 68.

14. Ibid., pp. 68–73.

15. *Business Week*, "The Relentless Pursuit of *Guanxi*," September 30, 1996.

16. "China's Economy at a Crossroads."

17. Ibid.

18. *New York Times*, "China's Inevitable Dilemma: Coal Equals Growth," November 29, 1995.

19. Ibid.

20. *New York Times*, "Right to Protest in Hong Kong to Be Cut Back," April 10, 1997.

21. *New York Times*, "Hong Kong's Legal System Braces for Chinese Rule," May 7, 1997.

22. Ibid.

23. Kenneth Kasa, "Post-1997 Hong Kong: A View from the Financial Markets," *Federal Reserve Bank of San Francisco (FRBSF) Economic Letter*, no. 96-35, November 29, 1996.

12

Conclusion

Economic performance and standards of living vary considerably across nations, and the gap between many rich and poor nations is widening. Many theories have been proposed to explain this phenomenon, including dependency theory and neoclassical growth theory. Dependency theory is limited in its usefulness, however, because it offers no internal introspection. The problems of developing economies are blamed on the core nations. Moreover, the policy prescription of import substitution advocated by dependency theory seems to have worsened economic performance in many nations. Neoclassical growth theory describes but does not explain the process of growth. Moreover, it predicts convergence of living standards, a trend that we simply do not observe in the real world.[1]

Institutions are the key factor in determining a nation's economic performance. Ronald Coase first directed attention to institutions by observing that the exchange process is costly. Transaction costs—that is, the costs of negotiating, measuring, and enforcing contracts—are significant. Therefore, economic efficiency as predicted by neoclassical economic theory may not result, because mutually beneficial transactions will be forfeited. The Coase theorem holds that only in a world of zero transaction costs will the efficient outcome prevail. Therefore, the primary goal of every economy is to create an environment with low costs of transacting.

It is the institutional framework of a nation that determines the level of transaction costs. The institutional framework consists of the nation's formal and informal rules and the enforcement mechanisms. Formal rules are the written rules of society; informal rules are the unwritten codes of conduct. Institutions can lower transaction costs by clearly defining property rights to the goods and services being exchanged so that measurement and enforcement costs are lowered. If a dispute arises in an exchange, procedures and judicial organizations are in place to resolve it.

Holding technology constant, firms that operate in a low-transaction-cost environment can specialize and divide their production processes. Firms focus on one narrow production process and use the market to purchase the necessary input. Specialization and division of labor lead to higher levels of productivity and hence higher levels of output and income. With a fixed level of technology, a nation will approach its production possibilities frontier only by having an institutional framework that results in low transaction costs.

Over time, a nation increases its wealth via technological advancements. For this to occur, a nation's institutional framework must promote the process of creative destruction, which forces firms to improve their products and technology over time or be driven out of business by a competitor. Many nations do not generate this dynamic growth because their organizations are permitted to remain inefficient, shielded from domestic or international competition.

The final piece of the puzzle is to understand how a nation's institutions are created. Most formal institutions derive from the political sector. In order to produce efficient institutions, the polity must be organized in such a way that markets are encouraged and protected. Market-preserving federalism is one type of political system that allows markets to prosper by fostering competition for economic organizations at the subnational level. Subnational governments must satisfy economic organizations if they are to survive. Dictatorships and unchecked congressional bodies are less likely to produce such efficient institutions, because they are more concerned with pleasing powerful interest groups.

The decade of the 1990s is a time of unprecedented change in world economies. Dozens of countries have started the transition to capitalism, and many developing economies are making serious reform attempts. We have explored the New Institutional Economics and applied the theory to transition and developing economies. Transition economies face the challenge of stabilizing their macroeconomics and revamping their entire institutional framework to facilitate market exchanges. Some economies, such as those of Poland, eastern Germany, the Czech Republic, and Hungary, are doing quite well. Others, including those of Russia and most of the former Soviet republics, are not. The difference is that the more successful nations have been able to create institutions that create the right incentives for organizations to conduct business. But in Russia, for example, that environment is not present.

Developing economies must change their institutions to lower transaction costs and promote competition. Over the past five decades, many nations have followed inward-looking import substitution polices while others have adopted export-led policies. Both strategies have strengths and weaknesses, but the dynamic incentives of export-led policies have been much more powerful. Many Latin American nations that turned inward saw their economies stagnate while trade deficits worsened because of slow export growth. Many Asian nations, however, provided incentives for their firms essentially to flood the world with high-quality exports. Though the domestic economies of these nations suffered, the process of creative destruction, with all its technological benefits, was in full force.

Many different variations and varieties of institutions can promote good economic performance. Poland, South Korea, China, and Hong Kong have taken very different paths, yet each of these economies has developed institutions that have led to economic growth.

Most economies have not been as successful. Developing an institutional framework conducive to growth is difficult and often impossible. Three-fourths of the world's population lives in less developed countries. Given current population trends, this proportion will rise over time. This does not mean that we should give up. Indeed, understanding the important role that institutions play in economic performance is more important than ever.

Mexico has been attempting serious reform in recent years and there is reason for cautious optimism. South Korea and the other newly industrialized countries have been extremely successful over recent decades despite the recent Asian crisis. China is a middle-ground case where much reform has taken place, but there are serious issues such as the conflict between socialism and capitalism that will need to be addressed down the road.

Institutions matter. This book has described how they matter. The biggest challenge to each and every nation is to create an institutional framework that leads to good economic performance. The odds of success are not overwhelmingly high, but with further study of institutions, economists and other social scientists can make policy recommendations that will help to improve the living conditions of most of the world's population.

Notes

1. We do observe conditional convergence, or convergence across some countries during certain periods. But there are many exceptions to the rule.

Index